Hermann Kaufmann
Christian Lenz

Walter Zschokke

Hermann Kaufmann
Christian Lenz

Architektur Architecture
und Struktur and Structure

SpringerWienNewYork

6	**Einleitung**		6	**Introduction**
9	**Kultur-, Sport- und Tourismusbauten**		9	**Buildings for Culture, Sports and Tourism**
10	Friedhofkapelle, Reuthe		10	Cemetery Chapel, Reuthe
14	Reithalle Propstei St. Gerold, St. Gerold		14	St. Gerold Provostry Riding Hall, St. Gerold
20	Fahrradbrücke, Gaißau		20	Bicycling Bridge, Gaißau
24	Jugend- und Bildungshaus St. Arbogast, Götzis		24	St. Arbogast Youth and Educational Center, Götzis
28	Umbau Gymnasium Kloster Mehrerau, Bregenz		28	Gymnasium Mehrerau, Monastery Renovation, Bregenz
40	Umbau Kirche St. Peter und Paul, Lustenau		40	St. Peter and Paul Church Renovation, Lustenau
44	Umbau Kirche Zur Heiligen Familie, Feldkirch/Tisis		44	Church of the Holy Family Renovation, Feldkirch/Tisis
48	Apartmenthaus Lechblick, Warth		48	Lechblick Apartmenthouse, Warth
55	**Industrie- und Gewerbebauten**		55	**Office and Commercial Buildings**
56	Lagerhalle Kaufmann Holz-AG, Reuthe		56	Kaufmann Holz-AG Warehouse, Reuthe
60	Möbelfabrik Linth, Kaltbrunn, Schweiz		60	Linth Furniture Factory, Kaltbrunn, Switzerland
66	Ausstellungshalle, Murau		66	Temporary Exhibition Hall, Murau
70	Holzlagerhallen Metzler H. KG, Bezau		70	Metzler Timber Warehouse, Bezau
74	Biomasseheizwerk, Lech		74	Biomass Energy Plant, Lech
78	Impulszentrum Bregenzerwald, Egg		78	Impulse Center Bregenzerwald, Egg
84	Architekturbüro, Schwarzach		84	Architecture Office, Schwarzach
90	Zahnambulatorium VGKK, Bregenz		90	VGKK Dentistry Clinic, Bregenz
96	Spenglerei Rusch, Alberschwende		96	Rusch Plumbing, Alberschwende
102	Aufstockung Ivoclar, Schaan, Liechtenstein		102	Ivoclar Expansion, Schaan, Liechtenstein
108	Büro- und Geschäftshaus MONO, Dornbirn		108	Mono Office and Commercial Building, Dornbirn

111	**Wohnanlagen**		111	**Housing Estates**
112	Wohnanlage Neudorfstraße, Wolfurt		112	Neudorfstraße Residential Project, Wolfurt
118	Wohnanlage Ölzbündt, Dornbirn		118	Ölzbündt Residential Project, Dornbirn
126	Wohnanlage Dammstraße, Schwarzach		126	Dammstraße Residential Project, Schwarzach
130	Wohnanlage Weidachstraße, Schwarzach		130	Weidachstraße Housing Project, Schwarzach
135	**Einfamilienhäuser**		135	**Single-Family Houses**
136	Haus Beck-Faigle, Hard		136	House Beck-Faigle, Hard
142	Haus Anton Kaufmann, Reuthe		142	House Anton Kaufmann, Reuthe
146	Haus Fuchs, Langen bei Bregenz		146	House Fuchs, Langen near Bregenz
152	Haus Raid, Schwarzach		152	House Raid, Schwarzach
156	Doppelhaus Klosterwiesweg, Schwarzach		156	Two-family House Klosterwiesweg, Schwarzach
162	Haus Lenz, Schwarzach		162	House Lenz, Schwarzach
166	Haus Hagspiel, Höchst		166	House Hagspiel, Höchst
170	Haus Eggler, Wolfurt		170	House Eggler, Wolfurt
176	Zubau Hallenbad Hampl, Lochau		176	Hampl Indoor Swimming Pool Annex, Lochau
181	**Erneuerungen**		181	**Refurbishments**
182	Gasthof Adler, Schwarzenberg		182	Restaurant Adler, Schwarzenberg
186	Haus Geissler, Wolfurt		186	House Geissler, Wolfurt
190	Fachhochschule Vorarlberg, Dornbirn		190	University of Applied Sciences, Dornbirn
196	Motorschiff Vorarlberg, Neuer Innenausbau		196	Motorschiff Vorarlberg Interior Renovation
201	**Anhang**		201	**Appendix**
202	Weitere Werke auszugsweise		202	Catalogue of Projects
205	Auszeichnungen		205	Awards
206	MitarbeiterInnen		206	Collaborators
207	Biographien		207	Biographies

Einleitung

Introduction

Walter Zschokke

Die Stimmung im eigenen Bürohaus in Schwarzach, dem langen Großraum mit einigen individuellen Arbeitskojen, ist unkompliziert. Ebenso verhält es sich mit der Architektur, die hier konzipiert wird: Sie ist so komplex wie nötig und so einfach wie möglich. Hermann Kaufmann und Christian Lenz arbeiten seit Jahren sowohl individuell als auch gemeinsam. Das Gespräch zu aktuellen Fragen der Architektur findet in jedem Fall statt. Geboren in der ersten Hälfte der fünfziger Jahre, konnten beide von der Begegnung mit der Lehrerpersönlichkeit Ernst Hiesmayr profitieren, der als wichtiger Vertreter der österreichischen Nachkriegsmoderne an der Technischen Universität Wien und in seinem Atelier wegweisend wirkte.

Hermann Kaufmann, dessen familiäre Wurzeln im Bregenzerwald und im Zimmererhandwerk gründen, hat im alpinen Kontext mit seinen steilen Hängen, engen und weiten Tälern, schroffen und sanften Erhebungen ein untrügliches Gefühl für topografische Situationen entwickelt, wie an der Reithalle für St. Gerold oder am Heizwerk Lech ersichtlich wird. Einer prinzipiellen Verankerung in der Region entspricht sein Verständnis für lokalspezifische Bedingungen: Zu wissen, wo architektonische Zurückhaltung und Feinfühligkeit angebracht sind, davon zeugen die Arbeiten in Bizau, die Friedhofskapelle in Reuthe oder das Haus Geissler in Wolfurt. Dass er deswegen mit seinen Entwürfen nicht auch für Sensationen gut wäre, belegen die Hallenbauten für Murau, St. Gerold und Reuthe. Letztere macht zudem seinen souveränen Umgang mit riesigen Dimensionen und differenzierten Proportionen nachvollziehbar. An seinen mit verblüffender Planungsgeschwindigkeit umgesetzten Entwürfen wird das Tragwerk nicht zum konstruktiv manierierten Selbstzweck überbetont, sondern zu einem integralen Element der Architektur. Undogmatisch in der Anwendung der Materialien wechselt er von Holz zu Stahl, wo dieser sinnvoller und für die architektonische Gesamtwirkung besser ist, wie anhand der Tennishalle auf der Möbelfabrik Linth in Kaltenbrunn/CH deutlich wird. Seine Experimentierfreude führte zu eleganten Bauwerken wie der Halle in Murau für die Ausstellung

The atmosphere in the Kaufmann/Lenz office building in Schwarzach, with its long large room that features individual work carrels is uncomplicated. This is also the case with the architecture that is conceived here: it is as complex as necessary and as simple as possible. Hermann Kaufmann and Christian Lenz have worked as architects individually and jointly for years. Dialogue on current architectural matters takes place in any case. Born in the first half of the fifties, both were able to profit from the person of their teacher, Ernst Hiesmayr, who was a major proponent of Austrian post-WWII modernism at the Vienna Technical University and also pioneered this style with his office's work.

Hermann Kaufmann, whose family stems from the Bregenzerwald Forest and who started his career as a carpenter, developed an unequivocal feeling for the topographical situations created by the alpine context with its steep inclines and broad valleys and both rough and gentle elevations. This can be seen in the St. Gerold Riding Hall or the Lech Energy Plant. His fundamental sense of responsibility to the region corresponds with specific, local conditions. The work in Bizau, the Funeral Chapel in Reuthe or Haus Geissler in Wolfurt, are all cases in which architectural restraint and sensitivity are appropriate. The halls in Murau, St. Gerold and Reuthe all prove that his architecture is not a good vehicle for sensations. The last example also bears testament to his fine sense for huge dimensions and differing proportions. The supporting structures are not over-emphasized as affected stylistic elements for their own sake in his designs, which are realized with baffling speed. Instead, they become an integrated architectural element. Completely undogmatic in his use of materials, he switches between timber and steel depending on which of the two is better for the overall architectural impression. This is clearly evident in the Linth Furniture Factory Tennis Hall in Kaltenbrunn/Switzerland. His willingness to engage in experimentation led to such elegant buildings as the hall in Murau, which he built for the "Holzzeit" exhibition or the innovative Ölzbündt residential project in Dornbirn. With his clear architectural language, he even created convincing examples of demanding

„Holzzeit" oder die innovative Wohnanlage Ölzbündt in Dornbirn. Mit seiner klaren Architektursprache formulierte er selbst für den anspruchsvollen Einfamilienhausbau einige überzeugende Beispiele, bei denen allerdings maßhaltende Vernunft überbordenden Luxus zu vermeiden wusste.

Christian Lenz befasste sich in seiner Praxiszeit nicht nur mit Architektur, sondern auch mit Design. Der lockere Wechsel vom Gesamtkonzept zum Detailmaßstab, die diesbezügliche Sorgfalt und ein rationaler Umgang mit den gestalterischen Mitteln, der die Detailbearbeitung nicht in manirierte Detailverliebtheit abgleiten lässt, führen bei seinen Bauwerken zu subtiler Einfachheit. Sie sind in verbindlicher Weise sowohl in unserer Zeit zu Hause als auch in traditionalen Strukturformen beheimatet, indem ihr Erscheinungsbild zu ruhiger Ausgewogenheit gelangt, ohne in vordergründiger Axialsymmetrie zu verharren. Im Umgang mit bestehenden Bauten – sei dies die Kirche in Feldkirch, die Aufstockung Ivoclar in Schaan oder die Erneuerung der MS Vorarlberg – erweist sich, dass neu eingeführte Elemente nicht Rezepten gleich abgerufen, sondern aus Altem und Neuem individuelle Gesamtkonzepte erarbeitet werden. Diese geistige Beweglichkeit erweist sich ebenso als Qualität bei Neubauten mit eng gesetztem Finanzrahmen, denn es gelingt ihm, beim sozialen Wohnbau gestalterische Haltepunkte zu setzen, die identitätsstiftend wirken. Beim Materialgefühl reicht die Palette von Holz und Holzwerkstoffen zu Ziegel und Naturstein, aber auch der oft abgelehnte Sichtbeton findet unter seiner Hand zu einer verfeinerten Ausdrucksform. Nicht demonstrative Härte, deren Nähe zum Zynismus bekannt ist, vielmehr Verbindlichkeit im Neuen spricht aus seinen Bauwerken.

Es zeigt sich, dass der vermittelnde Charakter an den von beiden Architekten gemeinsam bearbeiteten Bauten wie dem Bildungshaus St. Arbogast, dem Gymnasium Mehrerau oder der Fachhochschule Dornbirn noch besser zum Tragen kommt, und damit das prägende Element ihrer Architektur, die von vielen aus den Augen verlorene Angemessenheit, ihren stärksten Ausdruck findet.

single-family housing. These projects are also characterized by the measured reason that tempers what would otherwise be an overwhelming sense of luxury.

Christian Lenz also concentrated on design during his years of apprenticeship as well as on architecture. The ease of transition from an overall concept to the details of scale, the careful and rational use of design elements and the careful creation of detail without letting it become an affectation, make his buildings structures of subtle simplicity. They are reliably couched both in our times and in traditional structural forms. Their appearance suggests a calm sense of balance without insisting on superficial axial symmetry. His handling of existing buildings such as the renovation of the Feldkirch Church and the Ivoclar expansion in Schaan or the MS Vorarlberg renovation prove that new elements do not have to lead to new methods. Instead new and old methods can be integrated in the overall concept. This agility of mind has been a useful quality in reference to new building projects on slim budgets, since it enables him to create new design waypoints even when working on community housing projects that foster a sense of identity. His feeling for materials covers the spectrum of timber and timber components as well as brick and natural stone and even includes oft-rejected unfinished cement. Under his hand, these materials become refined forms of expression. It isn't demonstrative toughness, which comes dangerously close to cynicism that his work expresses. Instead, it exudes reliable friendliness.

It is likely that the conciliatory nature of the joint projects realized by both architects, such as the St. Arbogast Educational Center, The Mehrerau High School or the Dornbirn Specialized College achieve even greater effect by focusing on the strongest element in their architecture, which many have lost sight of: a sense of appropriate usefulness.

Kultur-, Sport- und Tourismusbauten
Buildings for Culture, Sports and Tourism

Hermann Kaufmann

Friedhofkapelle, Reuthe

Cemetery Chapel, Reuthe

Die Pfarrkirche von Reuthe stammt aus dem 12. Jahrhundert. In erhöhter Lage sitzt sie auf dem äußersten Ausläufer des nach Osten ansteigenden „Ellenbogen", dem Bergrücken zwischen Bezau und Bizau. Auf der um Geschoßhöhe tiefer liegenden Terrasse südlich und östlich der Kirche ist der Friedhof vorgelagert, gehalten von einer mächtigen Natursteinmauer und durchschnitten vom Kirchweg, der von Osten her ansteigend das Plateau mit der Kirche erreicht. Im Zuge der Errichtung der kleinen Aufbahrungshalle, für die eigentlich nirgends Platz war, wurde die Friedhofsstützmauer in der gleichen Art in Naturstein mit Strebepfeilern verlängert. So entstand ein kleines Vorfeld für die in den Kirchenhügel hineingebaute Totenkapelle, zu der von Westen her auch eine neue Zugangstreppe angelegt wurde. Das flache Dach ergänzt wie bisher den recht engen Platz vor der Kirche nach Süden, an der Kante gesichert von angenehm zarten Geländern. Alle Maßnahmen erfolgten „sanft". Sie betreffen und präzisieren die Topografie und verbessern Benützung und Zugänglichkeit. Der eigentliche Neubau aus dunkel eingefärbtem Sichtbeton, dessen horizontale Nuten auf die Tektonik der Natursteinmauern antworten, öffnet sich mit zwei gläsernen Türen nach Süden. Nach Osten empfängt eine Glaswand das Morgenlicht und die Blicke der vom Friedhof herkommenden Trauernden. Das Innere ist karg und feierlich zugleich. Die Wände in hellem Sichtbeton kontrastieren zum Holzpflaster des Bodens sowie zur abstrahiert baldachinartigen Decke aus Lärchenholzleisten. Diesen Kontext nobilitiert der schwarze, weiß geäderte Marmor aus einem Bruch bei Mellau, den Herbert Meusburger für den Katafalk und die Stele mit dem ewigen Licht wählte. An dem kleinen Bauwerk erweisen sich Geländefühligkeit und Sorgfalt im Umgang mit gewohnten und daher wesentlichen Elementen im öffentlichen Raum eines Dorfes, ohne dass auf einen zeitgenössischen Ausdruck verzichtet worden wäre. Auch vermeidet die rationale Anlage jeden Anflug süßlicher Kitschigkeit, wie sie in ländlichen Gebieten nicht selten Ausdruck gestalterischer Ratlosigkeit ist.

Reuthe Parish Church was built in the 12th century. It is located on an elevated site on the furthest extension of the "Ellenbogen" (elbow), the back mountain slope between Bezau and Bizau. The cemetery is on the terrace spreading east and south, one level beneath the church. The terrace is supported by an imposing natural stone wall and intersected by the church road, which reaches the church from the east, following the gradual slope to the church's plateau. The supporting cemetery wall was extended using the same type of natural stone and support columns during the construction of the small funeral parlor, for which there actually wasn't any space. Thus a small forecourt was created for the cemetery chapel that was built directly into the church hill, which offers access via a new staircase from the west. The flat roof supplements the rather narrow space in front of the south side of the church the way it always has and is secured with pleasantly delicate railings along the edge. All these measures were implemented "gently." They affect and delineate the topography more precisely and improve the facility's usability and accessibility. The actual new building is made of darkly colored, unfinished cement whose horizontal indentations correspond to the tectonics of the natural stone walls. Its two glass doors open to the south. A glass wall facing east welcomes the morning and lies within the view of mourners coming from the cemetery. The interior is simultaneously bleak and ceremonial. The pale, unfinished cement walls contrast with the timber cobblestone floors and the canopy-like roof made of larch wood slats. This structural context ennobles the black, white-veined marble from a quarry close to Mellau, which Herbert Meusburger chose for the catafalque and stele of Eternal Light. This structure shows a feeling for the terrain and careful use of the customary and therefore primary elements in a village's public space without losing sight of contemporary expression. The rational complex also avoids any sweet, kitschy departures, which are often found in rural areas and demonstrate a sense of helplessness in terms of design and expression.

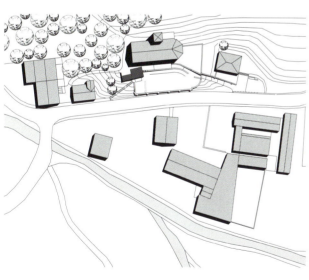

1995
Reuthe, Austria
Bauherrschaft | Client: Katholische Pfarrgemeinde Reuthe
Mitarbeit | Assistence: Alois Ratz
Kunst am Bau | Artwork: Herbert Meusburger
Publikation | Publication: Beton Zement, Technik und Architektur, 2/1996

12 Kultur-, Sport- und Tourismusbauten   Buildings for Culture, Sports and Tourism

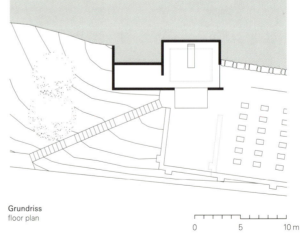

Grundriss
floor plan

Kultur-, Sport- und Tourismusbauten — Buildings for Culture, Sports and Tourism

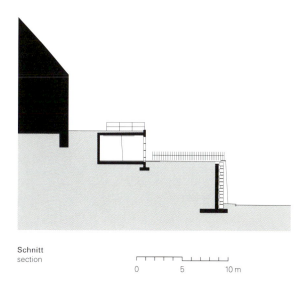

Schnitt
section
0 5 10 m

Hermann Kaufmann

Reithalle Propstei St. Gerold, St. Gerold

St. Gerold Provostry Riding Hall, St. Gerold

Nach Jahrzehnten des Zerfalls sorgfältig restauriert, dient die Probstei St. Gerold heute als überregional ausstrahlendes Kulturzentrum. Gewiss war schon bei der Gründung die gut besonnte Hanglage an der südexponierten Talflanke des Großen Walsertals bewusst gewählt worden. Nach Abschluss der Erneuerung des Bestands sollte nun eine Halle zur Reittherapie für Behinderte und Querschnittgelähmte das Leistungsangebot erweitern und auch für die kleine Haflingerzucht Platz bieten. Der neue Baukörper ergänzt die südwestliche Ecke der Klosteranlage, sodass deren Gartenhof räumlich besser gefasst wird. Zugleich liegt er parallel zum Hang sowie zur bestehenden Scheune, und definiert mit dieser zusammen einen Wirtschaftshof. Das große, über den gesamten Neubau gezogene Pultdach folgt der generellen Hangneigung. Aus der Ferne gibt sich der Neubau daher gegenüber dem Bestand angemessen zurückhaltend. Im Inneren der Halle kommt es wegen der dreiseitigen Verglasung mit großen Scheiben und der flächigen Primärwirkung des Daches zu einer spezifischen Stimmung offener Beschirmtheit: Man erhält kaum den Eindruck, sich in einem geschlossenen Raum aufzuhalten. Denn dieser wird von der Dachkonstruktion nicht auf eine Achse zentriert, sondern strebt – mit den Ausblicken in die nahen Baumgruppen – hinaus in die Landschaft. Südseitig öffnen sich große Schiebetore zum umzäunten Auslauf der Pferde. Über dem breit kragenden Vordach zieht sich ein Oberlichtband durch, sodass die Halle besonders im Winter viel Licht erhält. Die schlanken Stützen sind zugleich die Steher der Fensterwände, deren einfache Verglasung diese dank geringerer Lichtreflexion durchsichtiger macht, als dies bei der heute üblichen doppelten Verglasung der Fall ist. So schützt die Halle vor Wind und Wetter, bewahrt aber das Gefühl, sich in offener Landschaft zu befinden. Eine Wärmedämmung konnte entfallen, das Temperieren besorgt jeweils die Sonne.

After decades of decay, the St. Gerold provostry building was carefully restored; it now serves as a supra-regional cultural center. It is certain that the sunny site on the south side of the mountain facing the Großer Walsertal Valley was the preferred location for the building when it was built. After the renovation of the existing facilities, it was decided to expand the complex to include a riding hall for disabled and paraplegic patient therapy. The building also offers space for a small Haflinger horse breeding facility. The new structure extends from the southwestern corner of the convent, framing the garden courtyard space. At the same time, its alignment parallel to the slope and barn on the other side help define the farming segment of the complex. The large monopitch roof extending over the entire new building follows the general incline of the slope. From the distance, this gives the new annex an air of restraint compared to the existing buildings. The interior of the hall is characterized by a specific sense of protected openness due to the commanding effect of roof and the large glass panels used on three sides of the building: the visitor doesn't feel he is in an enclosed space. This is possible since the building's space does not center around one axes, instead it strives outward due to the monopitch construction – by offering views of the groups of trees close by. On the south side, large sliding gates open for the horses to be able to exercise and graze on a fenced range. The broad, projecting canopy features a skylight, giving the hall ample amounts of light, especially during the winter. The slender struts also act as the window wall supports. Single-panel windows were used since they allow for greater transparency and less reflection than the generally used double-panel windows. Hence the hall offers protection from wind and weather, but retains the feeling of an open patch of land. Insulation was not required since the sun regulates the temperature.

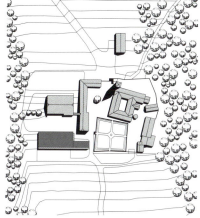

1997
St. Gerold, Großes Walsertal, Austria
Bauherrschaft | Client: Probstei St. Gerold, Pater Nathanael Wirth
Statik | Structural engineering: Merz Kaufmann Partner GmbH, Dornbirn
Mitarbeit | Assistence: Wolfgang Elmenreich, Reinhard Muxel
Publikation | Publication: baumeister 6/98; architektur szene österreich, Kapfinger/Zschokke

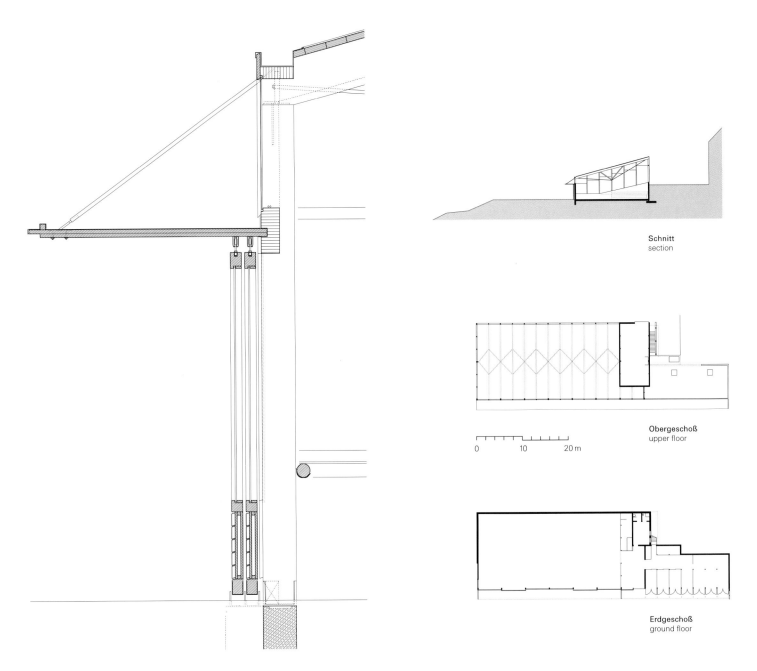

Schnitt
section

Obergeschoß
upper floor

0   10   20 m

Erdgeschoß
ground floor

Die Dachkonstruktion aus geneigten Brettschichtträgern, zwischen denen die Bohlen der Dachfläche zu sehen sind, wird in der Mitte von sechsteiligen Spreizen unterfangen. Die pyramidenförmig zusammenlaufenden Druckstäbe sitzen an der Spitze auf einem Zugband auf. Schwarz und dünn, treten die Zugstäbe aus Stahl optisch in den Hintergrund. So scheinen die Spreizen in einem paradoxen Schwebezustand zu verharren, verleihen aber dem Raum einen dynamischen Ausdruck von unorthodoxer Besonderheit. Ähnlich unprätenziös sind die gegen Winddruck aussteifenden Diagonalen innen vor die Glaswände gesetzt, sodass sie im Gegenlicht weitgehend ausgeblendet werden. Holz und Stahl kommen damit nach ihren Möglichkeiten und mit klarer architektonischer Absicht zum Einsatz.

The roof construction, which consists of bonded timber struts set at an angle between which the boards of the roof surface can be seen, is supported by six-part straddles in the middle. The converging, pyramid-shaped tension bars rest on the tip of a tension strip. The black, slender steel tension bars fade into the background visually, hence the straddles seem paradoxically, to hover over the room, giving it an unorthodox sense of dynamism. The diagonal elements set in front of the glass walls on the inside to provied support against the wind are similarly unpretentious, since they are almost invisible in back-lit conditions. Thus timber and steel are used according to their possibilities and with clear architectural intentions on this project.

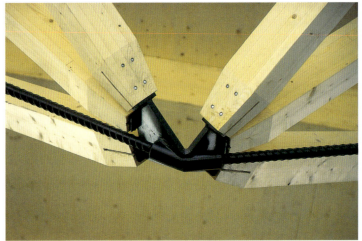

19 Kultur-, Sport- und Tourismusbauten   Buildings for Culture, Sports and Tourism

Hermann Kaufmann

Fahrradbrücke, Gaißau

Bicycling Bridge, Gaißau

Die Radweg- und Fußgängerbrücke quert den Alten Rhein zwischen Gaißau und Rheineck, zugleich die Grenze zwischen Österreich und der Schweiz, an einer historischen Brückenstelle. Der 45 Meter überspannende Kastenträger weist auf beiden Seiten ein langes Bandfenster auf, das den Brückenbenützern kontinuierlich Ausblicke nach beiden Seiten gewährt. Dennoch erfolgt der Vorgang des Querens in einem räumlich stark definierten Kontext: Wie bei traditionellen Holzbrücken handelt es sich um eine Art Brückenhaus, allerdings um eines in zeitgenössischer Ausformung. Man betritt dieses Haus durch portalartige Eingänge, bekommt dank der Aussicht auf den ruhigen Altarm mit, worauf man sich eingelassen hat, und wenn man das Haus wieder verlässt, steht man eben auf der anderen Seite des Flusses. Unter Bezugnahme auf eine kleine topografische Eigenheit, dass das Schweizer Ufer etwas niedriger liegt als der österreichische Brückenkopf, hat die Fahrbahn ein leichtes Gefälle. Der Entwerfer bestimmte jedoch die Dachkante des Brückenhauses als horizontale Gerade. Daraus ergibt sich ein schwach keilförmiger Zuschnitt der Rahmenträger, der vom Bandfenster aufgenommen wird. Als quasi kompensatorische gestalterische Maßnahme verengt sich die Fahrbahn leicht in der Gegenrichtung. All dies bewegt sich knapp an der optischen Wahrnehmungsschwelle. Nur die Formate der Brückenportale – leicht querrechteckig auf der Gaißauer und etwas überhöht quadratisch auf der Rheinecker Seite – sind deutlicher erkennbar. Damit wird der Nutzbau „Brücke" zu einem Bauwerk, das von einem subtilen doppelten Wahrnehmungsspiel begleitet ist: dem von Landschaft und dem von Bauwerken. Die Unaufdringlichkeit, mit der dies in den Entwurf eingeflossen ist, ist gerade für ein womöglich täglich von denselben Menschen benütztes Bauwerk besonders wichtig.

The bicycling and pedestrian bridge crosses the Old Rhine between Gaißau and Rheineck, which also marks the border between Switzerland and Austria, at the site of a historical bridge. The 45-meter long box-girder structure has a long ribbon of windows on both sides that offers bridge users a continuous view of both sides. However, the actual process of crossing the bridge is still completed within an emphatically-defined spatial context: The structure is a form of bridgehouse similar to those used on traditional timber bridges, but in a contemporary shape. One enters this house via portal-like entrances and becomes aware of the actual crossing as the old river meanders peacefully underneath, before reaching the other shore and leaving the house again. Taking the fact that the Swiss shore lies somewhat lower than the Austrian shore, the roadway was built on a slight incline to compensate for this topographical quirk. However, the designer created a horizontal plane starting from the level of the bridgehouse roof edge. Hence the wedge-shaped frame supports that are within the continuous ribbon of windows. Another more or less compensatory design measure is the slight narrowing of the roadway in the opposite direction. All of these measures are barely perceptible visually. Only the format of the bridge portals – slightly rectangular on the Gaißau side and a high square on the Rhine side – can be recognized clearly. Thus the purpose-built "bridge" becomes a structure that is accompanied by a double sense of perception: it is both part of the landscape and part of the structural development. The unobtrusiveness that is part of the design is particularly important for a structure that is quite possibly used by the same persons everyday.

1999
Gaißau, Austria
Bauherrschaft | Client: Amt der Vorarlberger Landesregierung, Bregenz
Statik | Structural engineering: Frank Dickbauer, Frastanz
Mitarbeit | Assistence: Martin Rümmele
Publikation | Publication: pro:Holz, zuschnitt 02/2001

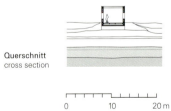

Querschnitt
cross section

0 10 20 m

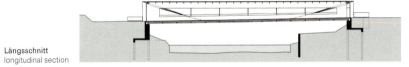

Längsschnitt
longitudinal section

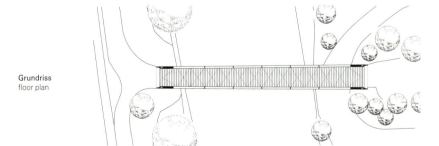

Grundriss
floor plan

Kultur-, Sport- und Tourismusbauten · Buildings for Culture, Sports and Tourism

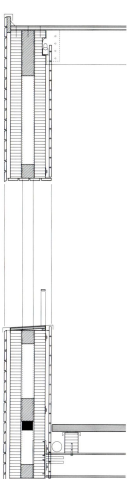

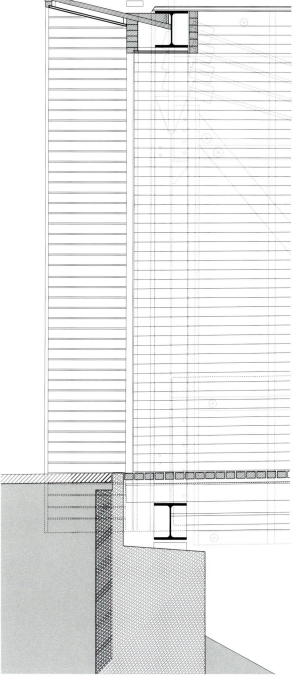

Das Tragwerk liegt nicht unter der Fahrbahn, sondern um diese herum, sodass es unmittelbar durch seine räumliche Struktur hindurch begangen und befahren wird. Die Untergurte der beiden unterspannten Rahmen tragen den Fahr- und Gehweg. Die Obergurte, zugleich Druckstäbe, werden von schlanken Stahlprofilrohren abgestützt und in durchlaufende Felder geteilt. Die konstruktive Scheibe der Dachfläche verbessert ihre Knicksteifigkeit. Die Unterspannung aus gebündelten Stahlbändern fächert sich im sichtbaren Teil in den Randfeldern des langen Fensters auf. Dies dient einer besseren Verankerung und Lastverteilung auf den Obergurt. Gegen die seitlich ansetzenden Windkräfte liegt unter der Fahrbahn ein Stahlfachwerk. Als Verschleißschicht dienen kräftige, gerillte Eichenbohlen. Die primäre Konstruktion der beiden Brückenträger aus Brettschichtholz wurde außen mit einer hinterlüfteten Rhombusschalung, innen mit Brettern in Nut und Kamm gespundet vor schädlichen Einflüssen der Witterung langfristig geschützt.

The supporting framework isn't located under the road. Instead, it lies around it. Thus visitors walk and drive through this spatial arrangement. The lower flanges and trussed beams carry the road and walkway. The upper flanges, which also act as struts, are supported by steel tubing and divided into continuous sections. The structured roof slab improves its torsion stiffness. The trussed, bundled steel cables fan out on the visible section along the edges of the long window. This contributed to improved fixing and weight distribution on the upper flange. A steel lattice was placed under the roadway in view of the side winds that act on the bridge. Strong, grooved ash planking was used for weather boarding. The primary composite wood bridge girders were finished with back-ventilated, rhombus-shaped boarding on the outside, while the interior planking was built with plough and tongue joints to offer long-term weather protection.

Hermann Kaufmann, Christian Lenz

Jugend- und Bildungshaus St. Arbogast, Götzis
St. Arbogast Youth and Educational Center, Götzis

Auf dem Weg von Götzis nach Klaus lichtet sich nach wenigen hundert Metern Fahrt der Wald zu einer ausgedehnten Wiesensenke. An ihrem westlichen Rand, in bester Aussichts- und Südlage, entstand in den sechziger Jahren die Häusergruppe des Bildungshauses nach dem damals verbreiteten Pavillonprinzip. Der winkelförmige Neubau aus den frühen neunziger Jahren besetzt mit dem Hauptbaukörper die Hangkante, wo er mit vier Geschoßen prominent auftritt, während der Nebentrakt orthogonal dazu nach hinten strebt. Bergseitig entsteht zwischen den beiden nur mehr zweigeschoßigen Gebäudeflügeln ein intimer Platz, wobei der signifikante östliche Kopfteil leicht einwärts gekrümmt ist, sowohl dem Gelände folgend als auch den Hofraum deutlicher fassend. Ein vor den Hauptbau gestelltes Dach auf schlanken Stahlstützen empfängt die Besucher und leitet über in eine weitläufige Eingangshalle. Die überraschend urbane Geste wird in einer langen Rampe vor dem Nebentrakt fortgesetzt, welche zu Kirche und Pavillons hinaufführt. Im Inneren des Neubaus bieten Speisesaal und große Aula im Obergeschoß räumliche Besonderheiten: Die Decke des Speisesaals wölbt sich in gestaffelten Flächen hoch zur Fensterwand nach Süden. Die Aula mit ihrer unterspannten Tragkonstruktion in Holz und Stahl verfügt mit Blick nach Osten über eine breite verglaste Öffnung, welche die Aussicht auf nahe und fernere Bergspitzen rahmt. Vor allem die Südfassade spielt mit dem Gegensatz von geschlossenen, weißen Mauerscheiben, durchbrochen nur von Reihen schmalhoher Fenster, und der großflächigen Leichtbaufassade in Holz und Glas. Das traditionale, im Alpenraum verbreitete Prinzip von bergender, massiver Sockelmauer und wärmender hölzerner Auskleidung, die im Bereich der Obergeschoße oft als Fassade nach außen tritt, wurde in den dreißiger Jahren bereits modern interpretiert. Von den Entwerfern aktualisiert, bietet das Wechselspiel von Schwer und Leicht in geländefühliger Interpretation außen ein klares Erscheinungsbild, im Inneren aber vielfältige Raumbeziehungen und -qualitäten sowie Aus- und Durchblicke.

A large depression in the meadow becomes visible after covering a few hundred meters on the way from Götzis to Klaus. In the sixties, the educational center's group of buildings was built on the meadow's western edge, facing south on a site offering a fine view. The complex was built in the pavilion style that was popular at the time. The angular new building erected in the nineties occupies the ridge of the slope, along with the main building. It is a prominent four-story structure with a lateral wing that reaches back orthogonally. The two-level wings share a small square on the side facing the mountain. The prominent eastern headpiece curves inwards slightly, following the terrain and framing the courtyard space for greater emphasis. A roof trussed on comely steel struts welcomes the visitor before leading him into the broad entrance hall. This surprisingly urbane impression is accentuated by a long ramp next to the lateral wing that takes the visitor up to the church and pavilions. The annex's interiors contain the refectory and large aularian hall, which are characterized by spatial particularities: The staggered refectory roof surface arches up to the southern window panels. The aularian hall on its trussed, wood/steel load-bearing structure offers a view to the east over a wide glass-clad opening that frames the scenic vista with its peaks both far and near. It is primarily the southern façade that plays with the closed white wall sections that are only interrupted by rows of narrow tall windows and the large, timber and glass lightweight façade structure. The traditional, widespread alpine construction principle of building a massive, protective base course with timber insulating cladding that was often exposed and acted as a façade on the upper levels of a building was reinterpreted in a modern manner as early as the thirties. Updated by the designing architects, this juxtaposition of heavy and light terrain-sensitive interpretations creates a cohesive exterior appearance. This is contrasted by the building's versatile interior spatial correlations and qualities as well as the views of both the landscape and of the facility's interior.

1993
Götzis, Austria
Bauherrschaft | Client: Diözese Feldkirch
Mitarbeit | Assistence: Peter Hafner, Albert Rüf
Publikation | Publication: baumeister, 1/1996;
Architektur & Bauforum, 5 – 7/1997; Gastlich Bauen, Prospekt

26 Kultur-, Sport- und Tourismusbauten Buildings for Culture, Sports and Tourism

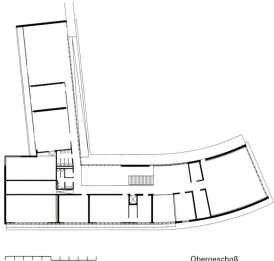

Obergeschoß
upper floor

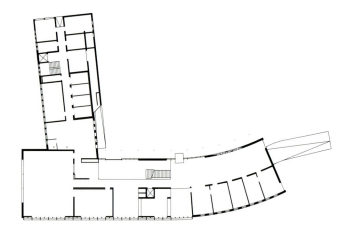

Erdgeschoß
ground floor

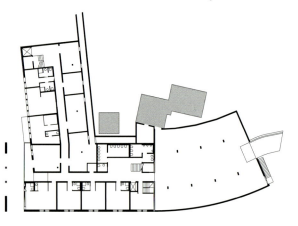

Untergeschoß
basement

Kultur-, Sport- und Tourismusbauten Buildings for Culture, Sports and Tourism

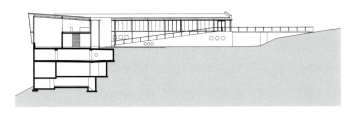

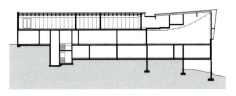

Längsschnitt
longitudinal section

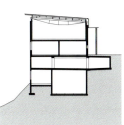

Querschnitt Eingang
cross section entrance

Querschnitt Mehrzwecksaal
cross section multi-purpose hall

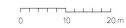

Hermann Kaufmann, Christian Lenz

Umbau Gymnasium Kloster Mehrerau, Bregenz

Gymnasium Mehrerau, Monastery Renovation, Bregenz

Das alte Zisterzienserkloster liegt am östlichen Rand des von der Bregenzer Ach im See über die Jahrtausende geschaffenen Deltas. Der kristallin wirkende Kern der ausgedehnten Anlage, bestehend aus Kirche, Kreuzgang und Zellentrakten, wird im Westen von einem großen, schräg zu deren Ordnung liegenden Winkelbau gefasst, sodass dazwischen ein weiträumiger offener Hof entsteht. Nordwestlich schließen ehemalige Ökonomiegebäude an. Mehrere Trakte werden seit Jahrzehnten zu Unterrichtszwecken genutzt, genügten jedoch den geänderten Anforderungen nicht mehr. Es galt daher, einen baufälligen Abschnitt in der Südfront zu ersetzen und angemessene neue Klassenzimmer zu errichten. Mit seinem Satteldach fügt sich der Neubau in die Struktur des Bestandes; auch zieht sich das gemauerte, teilweise mit flachen Kreuzgratgewölben versehene alte Sockelgeschoß vom einen zum anderen Nachbartrakt durch, die den Neubauteil wie eine Klammer umfassen. Die Lücke füllt nun – nicht zuletzt, um bei dem schwierigen Baugrund Gewicht zu sparen – eine Holzkonstruktion mit großflächig verglaster Fassade. Architektonisch wird der Neubauteil zum zentralen Element dieser wichtigen Schauseite, deren spannungsvolle Asymmetrie trotz des linksseitigen, attraktiven Giebels dennoch auf den überwölbten Eingang in der ungefähren Mitte fokussiert bleibt. Hofseitig springt der breite Klassenblock kastenartig um etwa eine Schrittlänge vor. Vom gemauerten Bestand ist er beidseitig mit zart versprossten Glaswänden abgesetzt, hinter denen sich Ruhenischen befinden, über die Nordlicht bis in den Mittelgang hineingelangt. Die Vertikalerschließung mit Treppe und Lift befindet sich östlich der gewölbten Eingangshalle. Sie zeichnet sich außen nicht ab, da dies der ruhigen Linienführung der Fassade abträglich wäre. Der regelmäßige Rhythmus der neuen Fensterachsen folgt mit seiner Größenordnung der historischen Teilung, der im Inneren die Spannweiten der Gewölbe entsprechen. Damit werden trotz anderer Materialien und Leichtbau anstelle massiver Mauern die Proportionen gewahrt.

The old monastery lies on the eastern edge of the deltas that were created by Bregenz's Ach im See River over the course of millennia. The crystalline appearance of the expansive complex's center, which consists of the church, cloister and the modular wing is framed by a large angular structure to the west built at an angle to the center, creating a broad, open courtyard. Former commercial buildings lie on the northwestern end of the complex. Many wings had been used for educational purposes for centuries, but were no longer adequate for changing needs. It was therefore necessary to replace the dilapidated segment of the southern front of the facility and replace it with suitable new classrooms. With its double-pitch roof, the new structure melds with the existing buildings. The walled, base course of the building with its partially flat cross-vaulting stretches from one neighboring wing to the other, framing the new annex in the manner of a bracket. The space is now filled by a timber construction with a large glass-clad façade due to weight considerations on the challenging construction site. Architecturally, the new annex is the central element of this openly displayed section of the facility. Its exciting asymmetry nonetheless remains roughly focused on the center, despite the attractive gable on the left. The box-like classroom block projects roughly the length of a step into the courtyard. It is separated from the existing walled structures by glass walls featuring slender mullions. Small carrel-like niches for reflection are located behind them and the northern light shines past them to the central hallway. The vertical access possibilities, steps and an elevator are east of the vaulted entrance hall. This cannot be seen from the outside since it would detract from the calm lines of the façade. The regular rhythm of the new window axes follows the historical division of the building and corresponds to the width of the interior vaulting. This helps maintain the proportions of the complex despite the use of alternative materials and light construction techniques as opposed to solid walls.

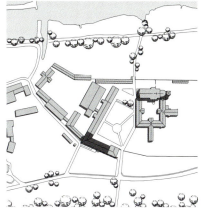

1997
Bregenz, Austria
Bauherrschaft | Client: Collegium Bernardi, Kloster Mehrerau
Statik | Structural engineering: Merz Kaufmann Partner GmbH, Dornbirn; M+G Ingenieure, Feldkirch
Mitarbeit | Assistence: Rolf Ennulat, Nives Pavkovic, Elmar Gmeiner
Publikation | Publication: Meherauer Grüße, Sonderheft 74, 1997;
Mehrgeschoßiger Holzhausbau, Ott Verlag, Thun, 1997; Architektur Aktuell, 221, Oktober 1998;
Architektur Aktuell, 227, April 1999; 4 x 100 Holzbaubeispiele

Dachgeschoß
top floor

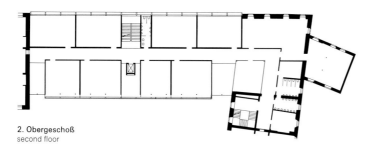

2. Obergeschoß
second floor

1. Obergeschoß
first floor

Querschnitt
cross section

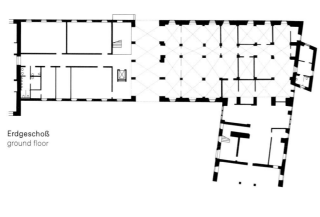

Erdgeschoß
ground floor

0   10   20 m

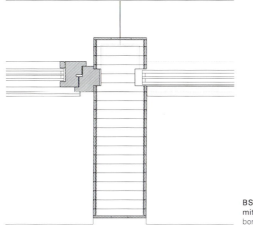

BSH-Stütze Fichte
mit Aufschwartung Eiche 7 mm
bonded timber support with ash veneer

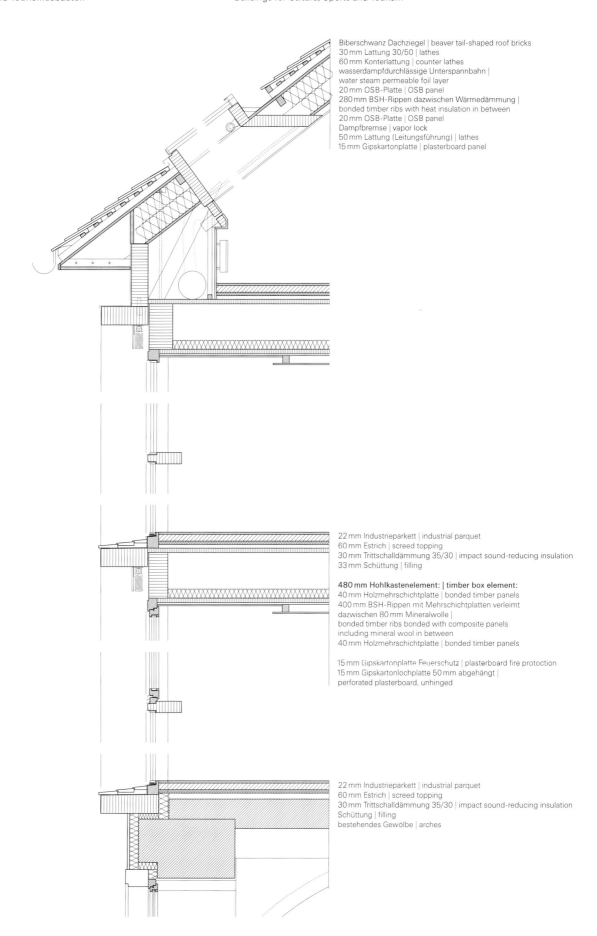

Biberschwanz Dachziegel | beaver tail-shaped roof bricks
30 mm Lattung 30/50 | lathes
60 mm Konterlattung | counter lathes
wasserdampfdurchlässige Unterspannbahn |
water steam permeable foil layer
20 mm OSB-Platte | OSB panel
280 mm BSH-Rippen dazwischen Wärmedämmung |
bonded timber ribs with heat insulation in between
20 mm OSB-Platte | OSB panel
Dampfbremse | vapor lock
50 mm Lattung (Leitungsführung) | lathes
15 mm Gipskartonplatte | plasterboard panel

22 mm Industrieparkett | industrial parquet
60 mm Estrich | screed topping
30 mm Trittschalldämmung 35/30 | impact sound-reducing insulation
33 mm Schüttung | filling

480 mm Hohlkastenelement: | timber box element:
40 mm Holzmehrschichtplatte | bonded timber panels
400 mm BSH-Rippen mit Mehrschichtplatten verleimt
dazwischen 80 mm Mineralwolle |
bonded timber ribs bonded with composite panels
including mineral wool in between
40 mm Holzmehrschichtplatte | bonded timber panels

15 mm Gipskartonplatte Feuerschutz | plasterboard fire protection
15 mm Gipskartonlochplatte 50 mm abgehängt |
perforated plasterboard, unhinged

22 mm Industrieparkett | industrial parquet
60 mm Estrich | screed topping
30 mm Trittschalldämmung 35/30 | impact sound-reducing insulation
Schüttung | filling
bestehendes Gewölbe | arches

Biberschwanz Dachziegel | beaver tail-shaped roof bricks
30 mm Lattung 30/50
60 mm Konterlattung | counter lathes
wasserdampfdurchlässige Unterspannbahn | water steam permeable foil layer
20 mm OSB-Platte | OSB panel
280 mm BSH-Rippen dazwischen Wärmedämmung | bonded timber ribs with heat insulation in between
20 mm OSB-Platte | OSB panel
Dampfbremse | vapor lock
50 mm Lattung (Leitungsführung) | lathes
15 mm Gipskartonplatte | plasterboard panel

Die Primärkonstruktion aus Brettschichtholz weist südseitig ein Rahmenwerk aus Stützen und horizontalen Trägern auf, an dem die kräftigen Hohlkastenelemente der Decken ansetzen. Nordseitig kragt der Raum aus, die Lasten werden mit schlanken Stahlstützen auf die Sockelmauer abgetragen. Während das Dach die gesamte Trakttiefe überspannt, sind die Hohlkastendecken auf Stahlprofile abgestützt, die in den als Speicher dienenden Betonwänden zu den Klassenzimmern aufgehen. An der Fassade sind die Träger aus Fichte mit einer kräftigen Schicht Eichenholz überfangen. Sie dient nicht bloß dem äußeren Schutz, sondern verleiht dem Holzwerk einen dem Wesen der Gesamtanlage entsprechenden Charakter. Wo nicht Fensterflügel zum Öffnen vorgesehen wurden, sind die großformatigen Gläser direkt in Nuten der Fassaderahmen eingesetzt, sodass ausschließlich Tragkonstruktion, Sprossen und Glasebene das Gesamtbild bestimmen. Eine kontrollierte Lüftung, deren Kanäle in den Deckenhohlräumen verlaufen, versorgt die Klassenzimmer mit Frischluft.

The primary bonded wood panel structure features a frame of struts and horizontal beams that meet the roof's robust hollow box elements. The room projects outward to the north and the stress is absorbed by the slender steel struts along the base wall. The roof covers the entire depth of the wing, with steel beams supporting the hollow box roof. The steel beams converge with the cement classroom walls, which act as storage space. The façade struts are made of spruce timber featuring a thick layer of ash wood. This isn't only for exterior protection; it also gives the nature of the entire complex the corresponding character. Large glass panels were mounted directly in the fluting of the façade frame if they were not intended as opening windows. Thus the support structures, struts and glass planes define the overall image. A monitored ventilation system supplies the classrooms with fresh air via hollow roof channels.

22 mm Industrieparkett | industrial parquet
60 mm Estrich | screed topping
30 mm Trittschalldämmung 35/30 | impact sound-reducing insulation
33 mm Schüttung | filling
480 mm Hohlkastenelement: | timber box element:
40 mm Holzmehrschichtplatte | bonded timber panels
400 mm BSH-Rippen mit Mehrschichtplatten verleimt dazwischen 80 mm Mineralwolle | bonded timber ribs bonded with composite space panels including mineral wool in between
40 mm Holzmehrschichtplatte | bonded timber panels

15 mm Gipskartonplatte Feuerschutz | plasterboard fire protection
15 mm Gipskartonlochplatte 50 mm abgehängt | perforated plasterboard, unhinged

22 mm Industrieparkett | industrial parquet
60 mm Estrich | screed topping
30 mm Trittschalldämmung 30/35 | impact sound-reducing insulation
Schüttung | filling
bestehendes Gewölbe | arches

38 Kultur-, Sport- und Tourismusbauten   Buildings for Culture, Sports and Tourism

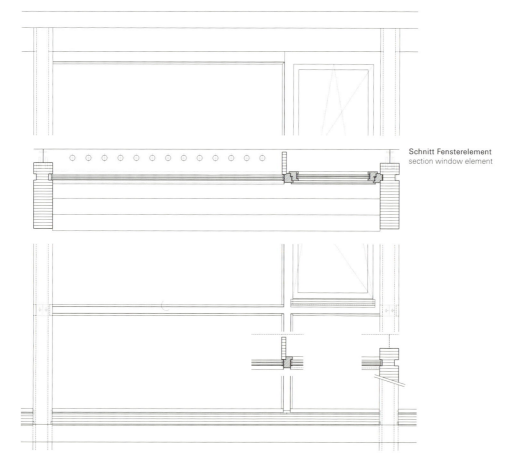

Schnitt Fensterelement
section window element

Hermann Kaufmann, Christian Lenz, Helmut Dietrich

Umbau Kirche St. Peter und Paul, Lustenau

St. Peter und Paul Church Renovation, Lustenau

Das wenig strukturierte Siedlungsgebiet der bevölkerungsreichen Gemeinde weist dennoch einzelne urbanistische Qualitäten auf. So wird am Kirchplatz die vom Supermarktdach und dessen Gegenüber evozierte profane Achse von der in Westost-Richtung verlaufenden sakralen Achse durchkreuzt, die nach der Weite des Platzraumes sich in einem langen, saalartigen Kirchenschiff fortsetzt und ihren Abschluss in der Apsis findet. Vor der Erneuerung waren die Innenraumproportionen eher gedrückt, und trotz hoher Fenster wirkte die Kirche düster. Außerdem litt der Einraum unter der ungünstigen Zonierung einer mittig an der Decke verlaufenden Flachtonne. Der Umbau veränderte die alte Raumstimmung radikal, sodass sie den heute verbreiteten Bedürfnissen nach einer Reduktion der allgemeinen Reizüberflutung entspricht. Die Decke wurde teilweise geöffnet und zeigt – wie in frühchristlichen Kirchen – eine eindrückliche Dachkonstruktion. Die Neuordnung der Liturgie und daraus abgeleitet des Grundrisses verlegt die große quadratische Altarinsel in den Bereich der Gemeinde, der sie an drei Seiten umschließt, während die Apsis zur Taufkapelle wird. Das Öffnen der Decke lässt indirektes Zenitallicht eindringen, das den Raum aufhellt und symbolisch das Irdische mit dem Himmlischen verbindet. Die Empore, deren Bodenplatte von den Seitenwänden gelöst wurde, verwandelte sich in ein frei hineingestelltes „Möbel". Der Entwurf führt zurück auf den durch Mauern und Gebälk gebildeten rohen Raum, in dem nun, von diesem abgesetzt, weiß dematerialisierte, schirmende Wände die neuen Begrenzungsflächen bilden. Damit wird eine Konzentration auf die geistigen Gehalte des Glaubens angestrebt. Dies kommt in der Gestaltung des liturgischen Mobiliars aus schlanken Stahlblechen, einer einfachen Steinplatte für den Altartisch und den dünnen Polsterflächen für die Sessio ebenfalls zum Ausdruck. Die scheinbar schwebenden Plattformen der Altarbereichsstufen vervollständigen die dichte Atmosphäre leichter, ihrer Materialwirkung entkleideter Elemente, die vom massiven Bestand aus Mauern und Dach bergend umfangen werden.

The zoning of this densely-populated community's residential area shows little structure, but it nonetheless has certain individual urban qualities. One example is the profane axle that intersects the religious axle from west to east at the church square, that continues as a hall-like church nave after the square before ending with the apse. Before the renovation, the interior proportions were oppressive and the church was dark, despite the tall windows. Aside from this, the interior also suffered from a poorly location of the flat roof cradle close to the middle of the ceiling. the refurbishment drastically changed the ambience of the room, so that it now addresses the contemporary desire for a reduction of general sensory overflow. The roof was partially opened and reveals an impressive roof structure, as was the case with early Christian churches. The new liturgical sequence and the ideas derived from it for the site plan are evident in the placement of the large, quadratic altar within the community, which surrounds it on three sides, while the apse acts as a baptism chapel. The opening of the roof allows light from the zenith to light the room and symbolically links the earthly and heavenly realms. On the other hand, the gallery, whose floor was separated from the side walls, was transformed into a free-standing, "piece of furniture." The design makes reference to the new bordering sections created by the removed, white and dematerialized panels around the rough space between the walls and columns of the church. The objective was to achieve a concentration of the intellectual contents of religious belief. This is evident in the design of the steel sheet metal lithurgic furniture, the simple stone slab of the altar and the thin cushions on the seating. The platforms of the stairs in the altar area seem to hover freely, thus completing the atmosphere of lightness created by the restained effect of the materials used on the elements here, which are securely surrounded by the massive walls and roof.

1991
Lustenau, Austria
Bauherrschaft | Client: Katholische Pfarrgemeinde Lustenau
Mitarbeit | Assistence: Peter Hafner
Publikation | Publication: Zeitung über die Kirchenrenovierung

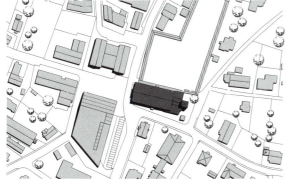

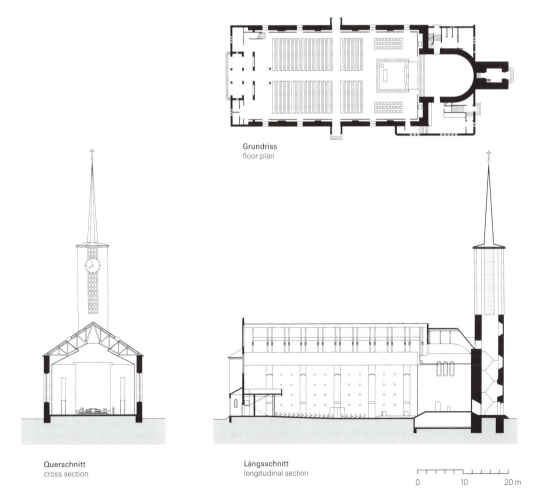

Grundriss
floor plan

Querschnitt
cross section

Längsschnitt
longitudinal section

0   10   20 m

Christian Lenz, Helmut Dietrich

Umbau Kirche Zur Heiligen Familie, Feldkich/Tisis
Church of the Holy Family Renovation, Feldkich/Tisis

Die vom Konzil beschlossene Neuordnung der Liturgie erforderte eine Adaptierung der aus den späten fünfziger Jahren stammenden Kirche. Der lang gezogene Raum von gestutzter Keilform und axialer Konfiguration wies die Mehrzahl der Plätze im hinteren Bereich auf und verfügte nur über geringfügige natürliche Lichtquellen. Das Konzept für die Erneuerung trennte daher den ehemaligen Altarraum mit einem transparenten Vorhang aus Metallgewebe ab und ordnete hier die Werktagskapelle an, die in dezidierter Querorganisation den Gemeinsamkeitsgedanken betont. In den solcherart bereits verkürzten, größeren Kirchenraum wurde im vorderen Bereich ein quadratisches Holzpodest für den Altarbereich eingesetzt, das von den neuen Sitzreihen U-förmig eingefasst wird. Durch eine Öffnung im Dach gelangt Zenitallicht in die aufgewertete Mittelzone. Ein Oberlichtband über der Südwand hellt diese auf und verbessert die allgemeine Lichtsituation in dieser Raumhälfte. Auf der Nordseite wurde mit einem transluzenten Vorbau die Eingangssituation neu gelöst, sodass auch von dieser Seite Licht einströmt. Matt verglaste Schiebeelemente ermöglichen, das Kirchenschiff vom Vorraum abzuschirmen. Mit den zurückhaltend gesetzten Maßnahmen wird der Längsorientierung eine vom Zugang und von der Lichtführung geprägte Querrichtung überlagert, welche die Raumorganisation für die neue Liturgie stärkt. Der Altarbereich ist nicht mehr axialsymmetrisch geordnet, sondern präsentiert sich als ausgewogenes Spannungsfeld, bestehend aus den Elementen Altar, Ambo, Session und Osterkerze. Von besonderer Wirkung ist jedoch der Vorhang aus Metallgewebe, dessen Gewicht von zwei Tonnen durch die Wirkung als zarter Filter für Licht und Blicke gleichsam aufgehoben wird. Seine auratisierende Präsenz verstärkt den sakralen Charakter des Raumes, verdeckt jedoch nicht die frühere Raumform.

The lithurgic reorganization decided on at the 21st Council of the Catholic Church made an adaptation of the church built in the late 1950's necessary. The seating was located at the back of the elongated and clipped wedge-shaped space. It also only disposed of limited natural light resources. The renovation concept therefore separated the former altar area with a transparent metal mesh curtain and located the day chapel here, suggesting an organization following the width of the structure, which underlines the sense of unity. A wooden podium was inserted in the altar area in this already shortened space that is surrounded by the new rows of pews in a u-shaped pattern. Light streams in from the zenith through an opening in the roof. A skylight transom along the south wall lightens the space even more and improves the overall lighting situation even more in this half of the space. A translucent porch structure provides a new solution for the entrance area, allowing light to stream in from this side as well. Matte glass sliding elements make it possible to screen off the church nave from the porch. These restrained measures layer a latitudinal orientation and organization of light over the former sense of longitudinal orientation, thus emphasizing the alignment of the new lithurgy. The altar is no longer defined by axial symmetry. Instead it is a place of balance tension composed by the altar, ambo, session and Easter Candle. However, the metal mesh curtain is of special importance. It weighs two tons, but its function as a gentle filter for light and inquisitive glances belies this fact. Its numinous presence emphasizes the religious nature of the room without concealing the earlier shape.

1997
Feldkirch, Austria
Bauherrschaft | Client: Katholische Pfarrgemeinde Tisis, Feldkirch
Mitarbeit | Assistence: Gernot Bösch
Publikation | Publication: Architektur, Städtebau, Design, Dietrich/Untertrifaller,
Springer Verlag, 2001; Baukunst in Vorarlberg seit 1980, Kunsthaus Bregenz, VAI, 1998

46 Kultur-, Sport- und Tourismusbauten   Buildings for Culture, Sports and Tourism

Kultur-, Sport- und Tourismusbauten — Buildings for Culture, Sports and Tourism

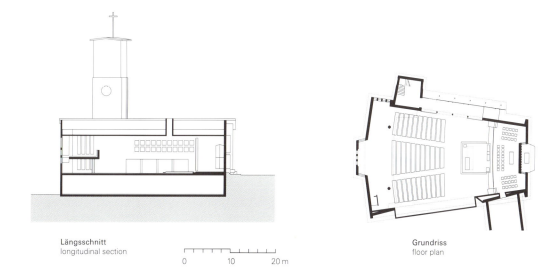

Längsschnitt
longitudinal section

0   10   20 m

Grundriss
floor plan

Christian Lenz

Apartmenthaus Lechblick, Warth

Lechblick Apartmenthouse, Warth

Am südöstlichen Siedlungsrand des Wintersportortes Warth sitzt das lange Gebäude exakt an der Hangkante, sodass die Aussicht aus den Apartments und von den breiten Balkonen nicht bloß zu den gegenüberliegenden Berggipfeln und nach Lech am Arlberg, sondern ins Tal hinunter und hinauf reicht. Den gerade geschnittenen Baukörper deckt eine Horizontalschalung aus geölten Lärchenholzbrettern. Nach oben schließt ein flaches Pultdach ab. Während vorn die Balkone sich dreigeschoßig über die gesamte Breite ziehen und beidseitig über die Hausecken hinausgreifen, wird die Rückfassade von den drei kragenartig vorstehenden Wetterschirmen der Eingänge rhythmisiert. Sie blicken auf eine kleine Gasse, die bergseitig von der ins Terrain eingetieften und erdüberdeckten Autoeinstellhalle definiert wird. Damit ist die Anlage in der Topografie gut verankert. Die Proportionen des Gassenraumes auf der Zugangsseite entsprechen jenen dörflicher Verhältnisse, während die Gesamtgestalt auf der Aussichtsseite auf Fernsicht konzipiert ist. Das betriebliche Konzept für die zwölf kleinen und zwei etwas größeren Apartments verzichtet auf den sorgenden Hotelier. Die Karten zum Öffnen der elektronisch gesperrten Türen werden den Mietern per Post zugeschickt, oder diese können sie in einem Herbergsbetrieb im Ort abholen. Im Übrigen sind die Gäste autonom. Die Konstruktion nützt die Eigenschaften von Holz und Holzwerkstoffen und verwendet Beton für schall- und brandhemmende Gebäudeteile, die zugleich konstruktiv aussteifend wirken. So bestehen die Stiegenhausschalen und die trennenden Scheiben zwischen den Apartments aus Stahlbeton, während für Außenwände, Decken und Böden Holz zum Einsatz kam. Es spricht viel Erfahrung und Ingenieurgeist aus dieser Konstruktion, die bis auf den Beton in Trockenbauweise ausgeführt werden konnte. Ebenso wurden die Treppen aus Holz vorgefertigt und als Ganzes von oben in die Stiegenhausschalen eingesenkt. Selbstverständlich galt diese Art der Werkstattvorfertigung auch für die Fassaden, die stückweise samt den Fenstern mit dem Kran in Position gebracht wurden.

The long building is located right on the ridge of the slope of the developed area on the southeastern edge of Warth, a winter resort town in Vorarlberg. Thus view from the apartment buildings' wide balconies isn't limited to the peaks directly in front of it and Lech am Arlberg, which is close by. Instead, it also allows for a view up and down the valley. The straight-section building is covered by horizontal larch wood shutters, and features a flat mono-pitch roof. On the front, the balconies cover the buildings' three stories and extend over the entire width of the structure as well as the corners. On the other side, the three neck-like protected entrance walkways give the back façade of the building its own specific rhythm. They open towards a small alley that is defined by the garage that was built directly into the surrounding terrain facing the mountain. Thus the complex is set well within the areas' topography. The proportions of the alley on the access side are in keeping with village construction practices, although the complete structure was designed to achieve its visual effect at a distance when viewing the prospect side. The operational concept for the twelve larger and two smaller apartments does not include a caring hotelier. Tenants receive their key cards to open the electronically managed doors in the mail, or they can pick them up at a hostelry office in town. The guests act autonomously in all other respects. The structure makes use of the characteristics of timber and timber structural components as well as cement for the sound insulation and fire retardant building components. These last parts also act as structural stiffening elements. The staircase revetments and the separating panels between the apartments are also made of ferroconcrete for this reason. Timber was used on the exterior walls, ceilings and floors. This building is characterized by a wealth of experience and engineering skill and it was completed almost entirely as a dry mortarless construction, except for the cement. The timber stairs were prefabricated complete units as well that were simply fitted into the staircase revetments from above. Naturally this form of custom workshop prefabrication also applied to the façades, which were put in place piece by piece, including the windows, with a crane.

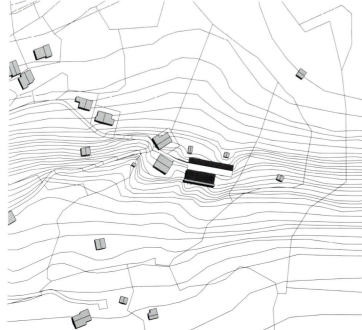

1999
Warth, Austria
Bauherrschaft | Client: Revital Bauträger GmbH, Dornbirn
Statik | Structural engineering: Mader & Flatz Ziviltechniker GmbH, Bregenz
Mitarbeit | Assistence: Helmut Brunner
Publikation | Publication: Der Standard, 17. 01. 2001; Die Presse, 16/17. 12. 2000;
Die Presse, 11/12. 12. 1999; Baumeister, 98. Jg., März 2001;
pro:Holz zuschnitt 5, März 2002, Nr. 5

Kultur-, Sport- und Tourismusbauten   Buildings for Culture, Sports and Tourism

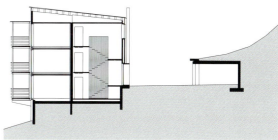

Schnitt
section

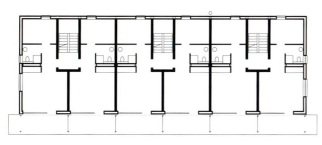

1. und 2. Obergeschoß
first and second floor

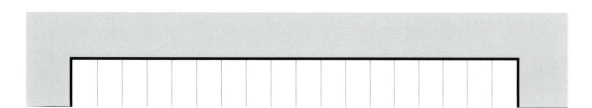

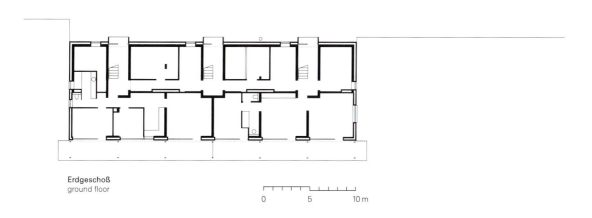

Erdgeschoß
ground floor

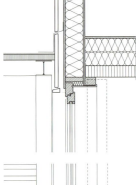

16 mm OSB-Platte | OSB panel
120 mm Mineralwolle | mineral wool
120 mm Mineralwolle | mineral wool
Dampfbremse | vapor lock
120 mm Brettstapel | bonded boards

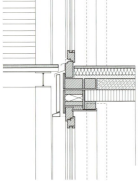

22 mm Lärchendielen | larch scantlings
35 mm Holzwolleleichtbauplatte
dazwischen Holzlattung |
lightweigt wood wool panel with timber
lathes in between
25 mm Trittschalldämmung 30/25 |
impact sound-reducing insulation
PAE-Folie | PAE-foil
30 mm Splitt | gravel
100 mm Verbundbeton | composite cement
120 mm Brettstapel | bonded boards

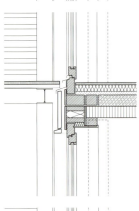

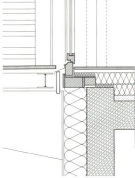

22 mm Lärchendielen | larch scantlings
Dampfsperre | vapor lock
35 mm Holzwolleleichtbauplatte
dazwischen Holzlattung, aufliegend auf Hartfaserstreifen |
lightweight wood wool panel with timber lathes in between, resting on hard fiber strips
2 x 100 mm Mineralwolle-Fassadendämmplatte | mineral wool façade insulation panel
40 mm Splitt | gravel
Flämmpappe | flame-heated bituminous roof sheeting
250 mm Dichtbeton | sealing cement

Die Konstruktion verbindet eine angenehme Raumstimmung mit hohen Wärmespeicher- und -dämmwerten und erlaubte mit Vorfertigung eine kurze Bauzeit. Die Decken bestehen aus einer schalldämmenden Holz-Beton-Verbundkonstruktion. Holz für den Zug, Beton für den Druck. Zuunterst befindet sich eine Brettstapelplatte, deren Unterseite bereits fertig gehobelt ist. Darauf liegt der armierte Beton, schubfest verbunden durch halb ins Holz eingedrehte Schrauben. Es folgen Splitschüttung, Trittschallmatten sowie Heraklith-Platten, dazwischen schwebend die Staffeln des Schiffbodens. Die Lärchenbodenbretter liegen auf dem Heraklith. Der Aufbau der Fassadenelemente beginnt von innen mit einer „Kantelwand". Hölzerne, auf Zug belastete Dübel halten die Bretter zusammen. Die gepressten und getrockneten Holzdübel gehen im Holz der Kantel auf und haften fest darin. Die Wandinnenseite ist gehobelt und somit fertig. Nach außen folgen eine OSB-Platte, die Steinwolledämmung, eine weitere OSB-Platte, die Konterlattung zur Hinterlüftung und die Außenschalung.

100 mm Brettstapel | bonded boards
16 mm OSB-Platte | OSB panel
160 mm Mineralwolle-Fassadendämmplatte |
mineral wool façade insulation panel
PAE-Folie | PAE-foil
16 mm OSB-Platte | OSB panel
40 mm Hinterlüftung | back-ventilation
30 mm Lärchenschalung | larch boarding

The structure combines pleasant room atmospheres with high heat storage and insulation values and prefabrication allowed for a short construction period. The roofs were completed with sound insulating, timber/cement composite components. Wood for tension, cement for pressure. At the bottom lies a composite wood slab, whose underside is completely flat. The clad cement lies on top and is secured against sliding with screws that are half-set in the timber. This is followed by a layer of crushed stone, impact sound-reducing mats and Heraklith slabs with the staggered ship planking hovering in between. The larch wood floor panels lie on top of the Heraklith elements. The façade detailing begins with a grooved wall on the inside. Wood tension-bearing studs were used to fasten the planks. The pressed and dried timber studs expand within the grooved timber, creating a firm bond. The interior section of the wall is planed and thus fully finished. It is followed by OSB paneling, steel wool insulation, another layer of OSB, the rear lath wood cladding for ventilation and the outer paneling.

Industrie- und Gewerbebauten
Industrial and Commercial Buildings

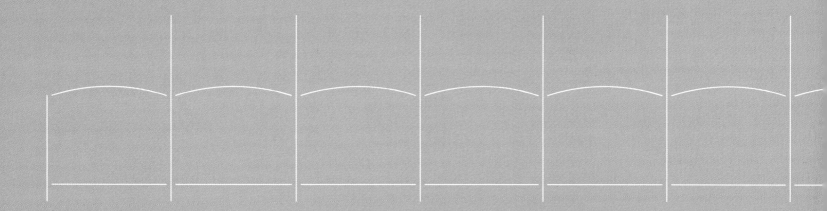

Hermann Kaufmann

Lagerhalle Kaufmann Holz-AG, Reuthe

Kaufmann Holz-AG Warehouse, Reuthe

Mehreren Hallen und Fabrikationsanlagen bilden den Industriekomplex, der ob seiner Ausmaße, weit drinnen im Bregenzer Wald, überrascht. Das sich verengende Tal und die nahen Bergflanken relativieren jedoch die großen Volumen. Die riesige Holzlagerhalle steht nahe an der Bregenzer Ach und bildet die Schaufassade der Gesamtanlage. Ihre flachen Dachtonnen und die Fassadenstützen geben einen Rhythmus mit dem Schrittmaß von elf Metern vor, eine Größenordnung, die den Normalhäusern in der Gegend entspricht. Dieses siedlungsbauliche Modul bietet einen nachvollziehbaren Maßstab, um den Baukörper trotz seiner Dimensionen im kulturellen Kontext einzuordnen. Die Reihung über 15 Joche und die Horizontalbetonung durch die gestaffelten Verdachungen mit Spanstreifenholz erzeugen ein kräftiges Kontinuum, das die landschaftliche Situation am Fluss aufwertet. Zwischen dem horizontalen, strengen Band der Fassade und dem locker darüber hinweggleitenden Wellenspiel der Dächer wirken die beschatteten Glasflächen der Oberlichter vermittelnd. Die Lagerhalle war nach einem Brand rigoros auf Zweckmäßigkeit, Ökonomie und Zeitgewinn geplant worden, dennoch kommen die Geländefühligkeit des Architekten und sein souveräner Umgang mit Proportionen und Maßstab anschaulich zur Geltung. Gerade wenn Standardformate von Holzwerkstoffen zum Einsatz gelangen, spielen deren Kombination und eine intelligente Umdeutung wie beispielsweise die durch Brettschichtholzrippen versteiften, gebogenen Furnierstreifenplatten der Dächer für den am Ende maßgeblichen architektonischen Ausdruck eine Hauptrolle. Das Ausnützen auch des knappsten gestalterischen Spielraums, den die statisch-konstruktiven Bedingungen zulassen, erlaubt, jene Präzisierungen selbst kostengünstigster Details vorzunehmen, ohne die ein Industriebau schwerlich zu Architektur wird. Nicht zuletzt erfährt auch das Innere der Halle mit der Rippenstruktur an der Unterseite der Dachtonnen eine Aufwertung. Die dichten Reihen konstruktiver Elemente bieten dem Auge Halt, die ungewohnten Raumdimensionen in Beziehung zu bereits gemachten Raumerfahrungen zu setzen.

A number of warehouses and production facilities form an industrial complex of surprising dimensions in the Bregenzer Wald Forest. However, the gradual narrowing of the valley and the nearby mountain range flanks relativize the large volume of the buildings. The enormous wood warehouse lies close to the Bregenzer Ach River and acts as the presentation façade of the entire complex. Its roof sections and façade supports are set in rhythmic, eleven-meter intervals, which correspond to the spaces between average houses in the area. This use of housing project-sized modules offers a familiar scale that allows the structure to fit within the cultural context despite its dimensions. The buildings' structure, which spreads across a framework of 15 straining pieces and its horizontal emphasis stressed by the staggered roof with its plywood tension strips create a strong sense of continuity, which upgrades the location close to the river. The glass surfaces of the transom that lie in the shadows seem to reconcile the stringently horizontal expanse of the façade with the loose set of wavy roofs. After a fire, the warehouse was conceived in strict adherence to timesaving, economic and purpose considerations. However, the structure is nonetheless proof of the architect's feeling for the terrain and his absolute confidence in dealing with proportions and scale. The combination and intelligent re-interpretation of standard-format timber components, such as the use of bonded timber ribs and the bent veneer panel cladding for the roof ultimately played a major role in creating the structure's overall architectural impression. The use of even the smallest design opportunity allowed by the structural/construction circumstances made it possible to realize even the most cost-efficient details precisely. Without this effort, it would be difficult for an industrial structure to be considered architecture. The rib structure on the inside of the roof vaults also help upgrade the interior visually. The dense rows of structural elements offer the eye a visual anchor, which allows the visitor to put the unusual spatial dimensions in perspective with respect to his previous spatial experiences.

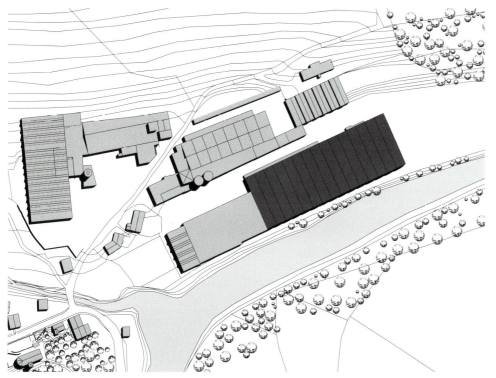

1992
Reuthe, Austria
Bauherrschaft | Client: Kaufmann Holz-AG, Reuthe
Statik | Structural engineering: Ingo Gehrer, Höchst;
Merz Kaufmann Partner GmbH, Dornbirn
Publikation | Publication: Architektur für die Arbeitswelt,
Birkhäuser, 1995; Holzsysteme für den Hochbau,
Kohlhammer Verlag, 1999; Architektur & Wohnen,
03/2001

58 Industrie- und Gewerbebauten   Industrial and Commercial Buildings

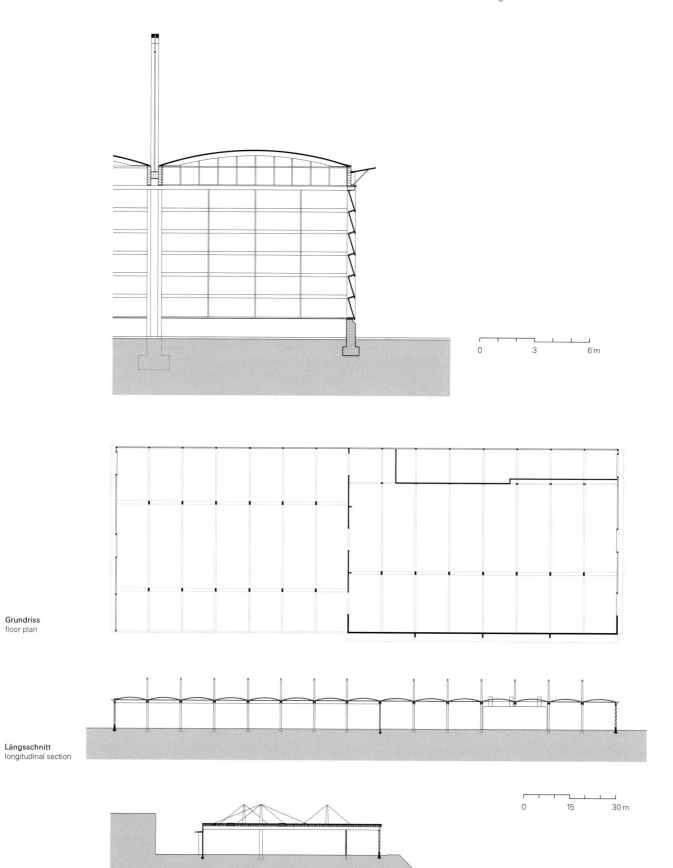

Grundriss
floor plan

Längsschnitt
longitudinal section

Querschnitt
cross section

Das Tragwerkkonzept zielte darauf ab, den Hallengrundriss nur mit wenigen Stützelementen zu beeinträchtigen. Zwei Reihen in den Fundamenten eingespannter Stahlpylone tragen die mächtigen, durchlaufenden Unterzüge aus Brettschichtholz, deren Feldweiten von Zugstangen unterteilt werden, die über den Dächern schräg von den Köpfen der Pylone herab gespannt sind. Wo das Dach nicht auskragt, sind in der Fassadenebene Pendelstützen aus Brettschichtholz angeordnet. Die Felder zwischen den Hauptträgern sind mit Platten aus Furnierstreifenholz im Standardformat von 2,44 mal 10,70 Meter überdeckt, die mit jeweils drei Rippen aus Brettschichtholz versteift und mit Stahlzugstangen zu einem Dachelement gebogen wurden. Für die Fassaden wurde Spanstreifenholz zu einem Faltwerk montiert, das Winddruck und Regen hinhaltenden Widerstand entgegensetzt. Hier finden Gestaltung, Kostendruck und ein nüchternes Verhältnis zu Holz und Holzwerkstoffen als periodisch ersetzbares Verbrauchsmaterial zu einer pragmatischen Beziehung.

The objective of the supporting structure concept was to only affect the site plan with as few supporting elements as possible. Two rows of encastré steel pylons carry the massive continuous bonded timber beams, whose open spaces are divided by tension rods that span the space diagonally from the pylon heads to the roof. The roof also features bonded timber pendulum-shaped struts for the non-projecting roof sections. The spaces between the main girders are covered with standard format 2.44 x 10.70 meter veneer slats. Each of these was stiffened with three composite timber ribs and bent into shape as a roof element with steel tension rods. A timber open-web girder structure was mounted on the façade to offer sustained resistance against wind pressure and rain. These factors create a pragmatic interplay between design, cost considerations and a sensible attitude towards wood and wooden components as periodically replaceable materials.

Hermann Kaufmann

Möbelfabrik Linth, Kaltbrunn, Schweiz
Linth Furniture Factory, Kaltbrunn, Switzerland

Der Hallenkomplex liegt in einem ländlichen Gewerbegebiet. Er umfasst, beginnend mit dem Untergeschoß, eine Autoeinstellhalle für über hundert Fahrzeuge und Verkaufsflächen; im Erdgeschoß eine Fertigungshalle, Flächen für Zwischenlager, Versand und Auslieferung; die Hälfte des Obergeschoßes beanspruchen eine weiträumige Ausstellungshalle für die Firmenprodukte – mehrheitlich Massivholzmöbel – und einige Büros, die andere Hälfte eine Tennishalle mit vier Spielfeldern und Garderoben; darüber liegen ein zweites Ausstellungsgeschoß, weitere Büros, ein öffentliches Restaurant, zugleich das Café für den Tennisbetrieb, sowie der Luftraum über den Tennisfeldern. Zuoberst befinden sich die Klimatechnik und ein flächenmäßig stark reduzierter Ausstellungsraum. Er ist mit den beiden darunter liegenden durch einen Vertikalraum mit attraktiver Treppe verbunden. Etwas bescheidener verfügt auch das Café über eine vertikale Raumbeziehung mit Galerie und Kaminzimmer und Zugang zur Terrasse. Von außen zeigt die nach Süden ortientierte Längsseite einen ruhigen, geschichteten Aufbau. Über den breiten Fensterwänden im Erdgeschoß stapeln sich in zwei Staffeln schweigende Flächen aus horizonaler Stülpschalung: die beiden Obergeschoße. Vorkragend das obere, das untere schützend und seinerseits beschirmt von einem Vordach, ist eine gleichmäßigere Abwitterung der Fassade zu erwarten. Schwertern gleich schneiden die vorstehenden Brandüberschlagsbremsen ins Schalungsholz, werfen scharfe Schatten und rhythmisieren die Fassade. Die Hauptzugangsseite mit An- und Auslieferung ist den verschiedenen Funktionen entsprechend differenzierter gestaltet. Der Hauptzugang in das repräsentative Stiegenhaus wird mit einem großen Rundfenster betont. Die dahinter befindliche Treppe – eine luftige Stahlkonstruktion mit hölzernen Stufen – hängt objekthaft in der hohen Sichtbetonhalle und wird von deren Kargheit stark aufgewertet. Den Großraum der Tennishalle dominieren die konkreten Skulpturen der Tragstruktur, die in klarer Hierarchie von oben nach unten mit einem Wechsel der Tragrichtung von längs zu quer den Raum aktivieren.

The complex of halls lies on an industrial estate in a rural location. Beginning with the lower level, it comprises a garage for over one hundred vehicles, as well as retail spaces. The ground level contains a production facility, mid-term storage spaces and delivery and distribution spaces. Half of the upper level is occupied by a large exhibition hall for the company's products – mainly solid wood furniture – and a few offices. The other half is the site of a tennis hall including four courts and changing rooms. Above the courts lies a second exhibition level, more offices and a restaurant that is open to the public, which also doubles as the courtside café. This area also includes enough airspace for the tennis courts below. The air conditioning and a very reduced third exhibition room are located on the uppermost level. This level is connected to the two floors below via a vertical space featuring an attractive staircase. The café is also characterized by a somewhat more modest vertical sense with its gallery, chimney room and access to the terrace. From the outside, the length of the building facing south displays a calm., layered structure. Two silent layers of horizontal weather boarding are set above the broad windows on the ground level. Since the uppermost level projects slightly above the middle level, which is protected by a canopy, the façade can be expected to weather evenly. The protruding fire retardant panels cut into the timber boarding in a manner similar to two swords, creating sharp shadows and adding rhythm to the façade. The main access side and delivery area were designed in a different manner in keeping with their varying functions. The main entry to the representative company staircase is emphasized by a large round window. The stairs behind it, an airy structure with wooden steps, hangs object-like in the high unfinished cement hall. Its effect is enhanced by the hall's bleakness. The concrete sculptures of the support structure dominate the large interior of the tennis hall by activating the space with its clear, hierarchical top down structure and the transition from a longitudinal to a latitudinal sense of support.

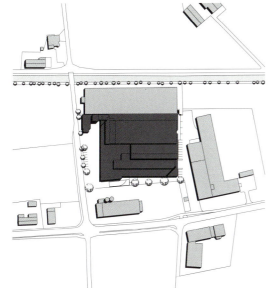

1995
Kaltbrunn, Schweiz | Switzerland
Bauherrschaft | Client: Linth Möbel AG, Kaltbrunn
Mitarbeit | Assistence: Alois Ratz, Jürgen Hagspiel
Publikation | Publication: Schweizer Baublatt, Nr. 89, 11/1994;
Architektur Aktuell, 197, November 1996

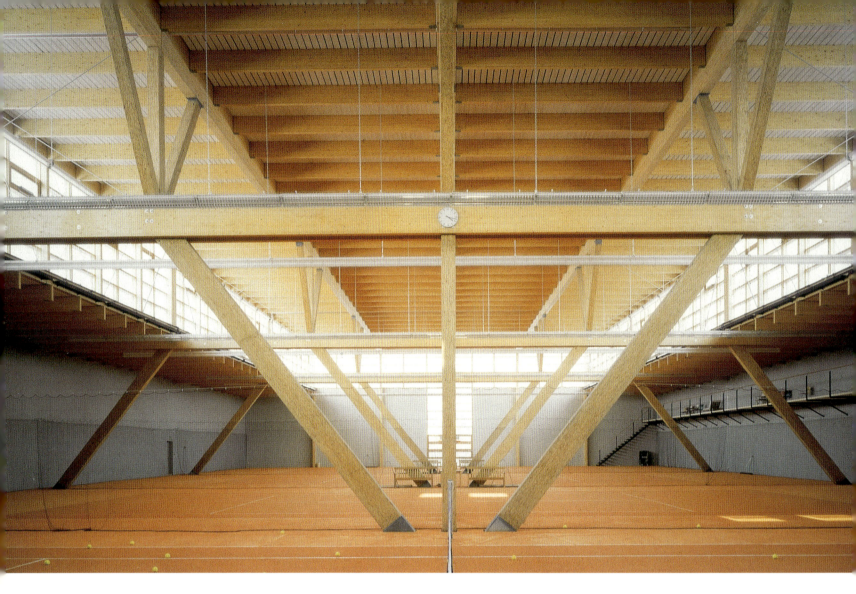

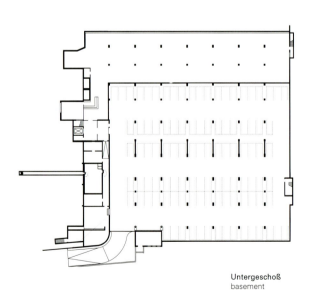

Untergeschoß
basement

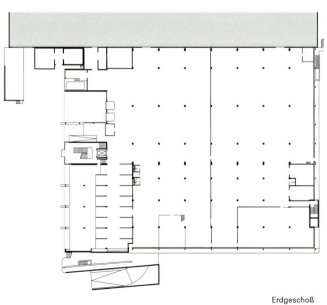

Erdgeschoß
ground floor

Industrie- und Gewerbebauten Industrial and Commercial Buildings

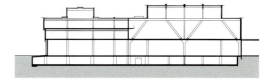

Querschnitt
cross section

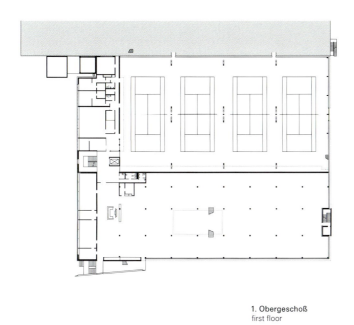
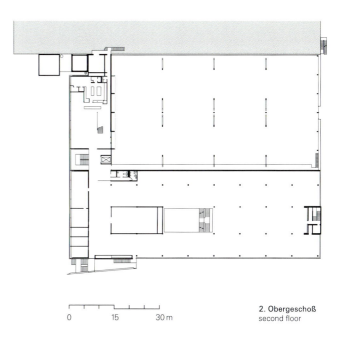

1. Obergeschoß
first floor

0 15 30 m

2. Obergeschoß
second floor

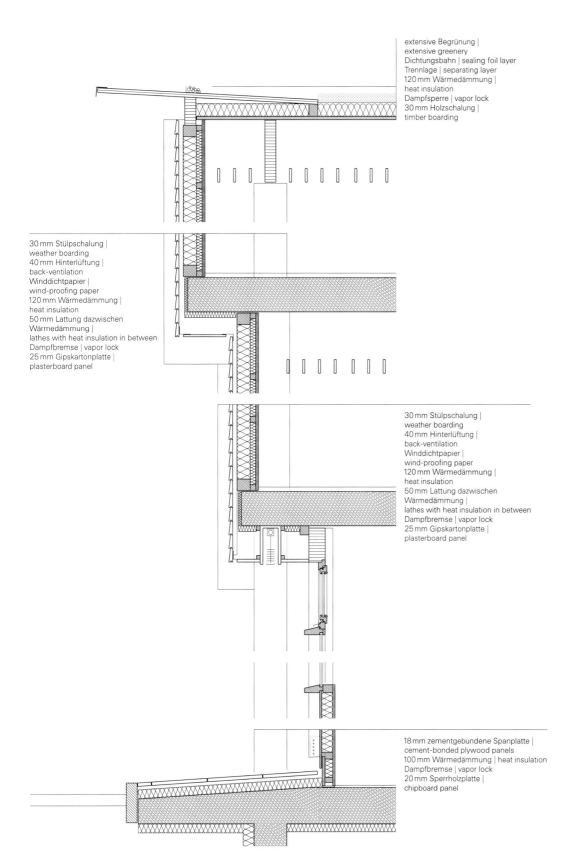

Das Holztragwerk des Tennishallendachs geht zum einen aus von den Stützenrastern der unteren Geschoße, diktiert von den Nutzungen; zum anderen muss über den Spielfeldern der Luftraum für Lobs garantiert sein. In der unteren Raumhälfte prägen daher kräftige Streben parallel zur Spielrichtung den Eindruck. In der oberen Hälfte wird das System gedreht, die Lasten von den Primärträgern werden in jeder Achse von jeweils drei Stäben gesammelt, was die Spannweiten des Durchlaufträgers verkürzt und auf einen Punkt konzentriert, wo sie von den Streben übernommen werden. Die Zugfunktionen in den Fachwerkträgern werden Zugstangen aus Stahl übertragen, die vor den Fenstern des Obergadens fast nicht in Erscheinung treten. Dieser Wechsel in Material und Dimension bewahrt den architektonisch-struktiven Aufbau vor einem Zuviel an massiven Stäben, die Raumeindruck und Lichtführung empfindlich stören würden. Ein Teil des Tragsystems wird damit optisch zurückgenommen und der Raumwirkung der Vorgang gegeben.

The timber supporting framework of the tennis hall roof springs from the grid of struts of the lower levels dictated by the buildings' purpose, although it was necessary to insure that there would be enough space for the players below to be able to play a lob. Therefore, powerful stays set parallel to the direction of play dominate the lower half of the space. This system is turned around on the upper half, with three rods absorbing the burden of the primary beams on each axle. This reduced the span of the continuous girders and concentrated the strain on points where it is absorbed by the stays. Steel tension bars bear the strain on the open web girders that are almost invisible from the upper transom. This change in material and dimensions prevents the architectural, structural concept from being overpopulated with massive rods that would disturb the spatial impression and light distribution considerably. Hence part of the support system was visually reduced, giving the spatial effect priority.

Hermann Kaufmann

Ausstellungshalle, Murau

Temporary Exhibition Hall, Murau

Der Entwurf für eine temporäre Ausstellungshalle aus Holz von 300 Quadratmetern Innenfläche, errichtet für die Steirische Landesausstellung 1995 in Murau, „Holzzeit", ging aus einem Wettbewerb unter fünf Architekten hervor. Dem klaren konstruktiven Konzept des Siegerprojekts entsprach ein ebenso einfacher längsrechteckiger, für unterschiedliche Ausstellungszwecke geeigneter Innenraum, der sein gedämpftes Licht von beidseitigen Zeilen hochliegender Fenster, von fünf shedartigen Oberlichtern sowie von den großflächig verglasten, mit Lamellen verschatteten Stirnseiten erhielt. Die beiden Eingänge waren raumhoch mit roter Farbe gekennzeichnet, alle übrigen Teile blieben naturbelassen. Beide Stirnfassaden verfügten über einen räumlich und konstruktiv mehrschichtigen Aufbau. Boden, Seitenwände und Dach waren kragenartig vorgezogen, sodass eine geschützte Loggia entstand, in die ein stützender und aussteifender Doppelrahmen frei hineingestellt war. Dahinter folgte die neutralisierende Schicht der horizontalen Lamellen, die einen Schleier vor die Glaswand legten. Zum Eingang führte ein langer, gerader Rampensteg hin, die anschließende Doppeltür war beidseitig von hohen, ebenfalls kräftig rot lackierten Mehrschichtplatten flankiert. Die Seitenfassaden wurden von den Versteifungsrippen in einem knappen Rhythmus plastisch belebt und von längsaussteifenden Vordächern beschirmt. Die querrechteckig proportionierten, hochliegenden Fenster verschwanden fast im Schatten dieser Vordächer beziehungsweise wirkten ähnlich einer Schattennut, über der das Dach, abgestützt auf den verlängerten Rippen, zu schweben schien. Der logische konstruktive Aufbau und die gewählten Proportionen verliehen dem Bauwerk trotz der banalen Großform eines einfachen Quaders bestechende Eleganz, was im Glulam-Award 1996 international Anerkennung fand. Für eine potenzielle Nachnutzung war vom Architekten bereits ein Konzept, die Halle wintertauglich nachzurüsten, ausgearbeitet worden. Nach der Ausstellung wurde die Halle an eine Gemeinde in der Steiermark verkauft.

The "Holzzeit" (Timber Time) design for a temporary wooden exhibition hall featuring 300 sqm. of interior space for the 1995 Styrian Provincial Fair in Murau was the winning entry in a competition among five architects for the contract. The winning project featured a simple rectangular interior space for various exhibition purposes. The structure's subdued lighting is supplied by two rows of windows along the upper section of the building as well as five shed-like upper lights and the large glass-paneled surfaces in front with adjustable slats. The two entrances were highlighted with ceiling-high red markings while all other parts were left in their natural state. Both street side façades cover multi-layered spatial structures. The floors, lateral walls and roof were built as neck-like projecting elements, creating a protected loggia that features a free-standing, stiffening double frame. This structure was followed with a layer of neutralizing horizontal slats, giving the glass wall an additional veil. A long, straight ramp leads the visitor to the double doors of the entrance, which are flanked by tall, deep red bonded panels on both sides. The relief of the lateral façades was heightened by a tight pattern created with the structure's stiffening ribs. These elements are protected by the longitudinal stiffening elements of the canopies. The long rectangular windows along the upper segment of the building almost disappear under the shade of these canopies creating a a shadowy depression over which the roof seems to hover on the supports of the extended ribbing. Despite the commonplace square shape, the building's logical construction and the proportions chosen for it give the structure its captivating elegance. This achievement received international recognition in form of the 1996 Glulam Award. The architect also prepared plans for the sustained, year-round use of the facility. It was later sold to a Styrian community for further use.

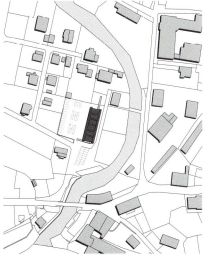

1995
Murau, Austria
Bauherrschaft | Client: Steiermärkische Landesregierung, Graz
Mitarbeit | Assistence: Thomas Mennel
Publikation | Publication: architektur-Bauen mit Holz, 6/1995

Industrie- und Gewerbebauten Industrial and Commercial Buildings

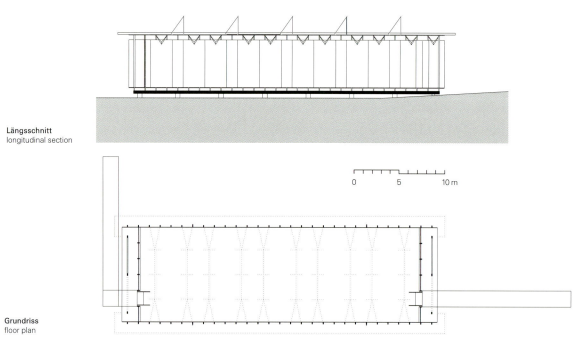

Längsschnitt
longitudinal section

Grundriss
floor plan

Die gesamte Konstruktion der Ausstellungshalle baute auf transportfähigen Elementen von maximal 2,40 Meter Breite auf, sodass Werkstattfertigung, An- und Wegtransport sowie Neuaufstellung an einem anderen Ort ohne viel zusätzlichen Aufwand möglich sein sollten. Die konstruktive Basis bildeten drei Streifenfundamente, auf denen eine Schar beidseitig auskragender Brettschichtträger ruhte. Die Wände aus Mehrschichtplatten waren mit schlanken Rippen versteift, deren Köpfe trugen das Dach. In einfacher Weise mit einer schlanken Stahlkonstruktion unterspannte Furnierholzplatten bildeten die primäre Konstruktion, jeweils unterbrochen von insgesamt fünf Oberlichtaufbauten. Die Queraussteifung übernahmen die ausgekreuzten Rahmen an den Gebäudestirnen, während die Vordachscheiben die an den Längsseiten anfallenden Horizontalkräfte sammelten und auf die steifen Rahmen übertrugen. Statische Logik, konstruktive Eleganz und architektonische Qualität fanden an diesem Bauwerk zusammen zu rar gewordener Harmonie.

The entire exhibition hall structure was completed using transportable elements no wider than 2.40 meters. This made workshop finishing requirements, transport to and from a site and setting up the hall in different locations possible without much additional effort. The construction was based on three continuous foundations fitted with grouped timber trusses projecting in both directions. The bonded timber walls were stiffened with slender ribs. The roof rested on the ends of these elements. Veneer wood cladding panels combined simply with a slender steel construction composed the primary structure, which was interrupted by a total of five skylight structures. The building's latitudinal rigidity was insured by the cross-shaped frames on the structures front and back façades, while the canopy cladding absorbed the forces acting horizontally on the building before transmitting them to the rigid building frame. Structural logic, elegance and architectural quality converge in this building creating a rare form of harmony.

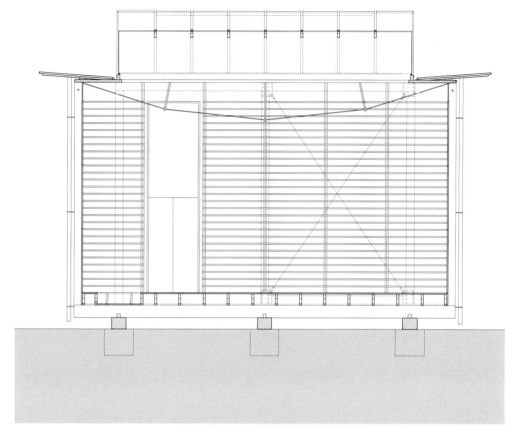

Hermann Kaufmann

Holzlagerhallen Metzler H. KG, Bezau

Metzler Timber Warehouse, Bezau

Die Halle und das große Dach befinden sich im Nahbereich der Bregenzer Ach in relativ beengter Lage zwischen Straße, ehemaliger Bahntrasse und einem Bach. Mit 30 Metern Spannweite bedeckt die Halle stützenfrei 2.400 Quadratmeter Fläche. Außen deckt eine Stülpschalung in traditioneller Weise den quaderförmigen Industriebaukörper. Darüber zieht sich allseitig ein hohes Oberlichtband, das von den feinen Linien eines Gesimses und des Dachabschlusses begrenzt wird. Ostseitig ist eine im Vergleich zur Halle kleine zweigeschoßige Bürobox unter das Dach geschoben, kaum größer als das riesige Tor daneben, sodass ein Spiel unterschiedlicher Maßstäblichkeiten anhebt: von der großen Öffnung des Tors zur Halle und von diesem zur kleinteiligen Befensterung der ebenso großen Bürobox sowie von dieser zum Tor und zur Halle. Das Innere des riesigen Raumes gewinnt durch die Form der massiven Fischbauchträger, die bezogen auf das Dach auch ohne vorhandene Schneelast zu optischer Schwere beiträgt, an Ausdruckskraft. Dazu im Gegensatz steht das leichte Oberlichtband, dessen Wirkung dank des Hochziehens der Untergurte zu den Auflagern an den Köpfen der eingespannten Stahlstützen nicht geschmälert wird. Auch wenn die kräftigen Profile unübersehbar sind, bleibt das Dach, einer schweren Wolke gleich, über dem großen Einraum gleichsam in Schwebe. Zusammen mit den Ausblicken unter dem Dach hervor durch das Oberlichtband auf die umgebenden Berghänge entsteht so eine Raumqualität, die anderen Nutzungen als einem Holzlager durchaus gut anstehen würde. Vielleicht noch ausgeprägter kommt dies bei dem später errichteten, aber weitgehend gleich konzipierten, seitlich offenen großen Dach daneben zum Ausdruck: Die Rundungen der Fischbauchträger lassen den Raum durchfließen, ohne ihn zu zentrieren. Der pragmatische, schräge Anschnitt des Rechteckgrundrisses mit der Mauer entlang des alten Bahndamms bildet einen Bruch, eine Irregularität und erhöht die architektonische Spannung.

The warehouse and large roofed space are located close to the Ach River in Bregenz on a relatively crowded site between the road, a former railway route and a creek. The hall spans 30 meters and covers a surface of 2,400 meters. Traditional weather boarding covers the square industrial structure's exterior. A skylight along the fine lines of the ledge and roof endings illuminates the room. Compared to the hall, a small two-story office box was placed under the roof to the east that is barely larger than the gate next to it. This accentuates the interplay of varying scales: it begins with the large gate opening and continues with the small windows of the office box and its relation to the gate and hall. The huge room's interior is given additional expressiveness due to the shape of the solid fish-bellied girders that contribute to the heavy visual impression even when not snow-laden. The effect of the delicate skylight is not diminished by the higher placement of the bottom flanges closer to the saddles on the heads of the encastré steel beams. Although the massive beam profiles cannot be ignored, the roof is nonetheless akin to a heavy cloud that seems to hover over the large interior space. Thus the quality of the structures' space, with the surrounding slopes visible thorough the skylight, would also suffice for purposes other than timber storage. This impression is perhaps given even greater emphasis in the construction of the large adjacent roof with its lateral opening: the round sections of the fish-bellied girders, which allow the room to flow without centering it. The pragmatic, diagonal ingate of the rectangular site plan including the wall along the old train dam creates an irregular rupture that definitely increases the architectural tension.

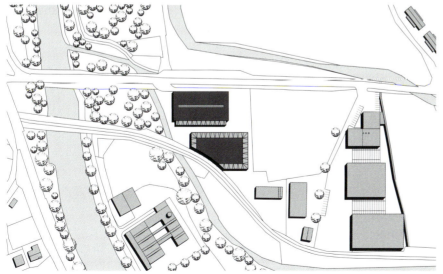

1997 und 2000
Bezau, Austria
Bauherrschaft | Client: Metzler H. KG, Schwarzach
Mitarbeit | Assistence: Jürgen Hagspiel
Publikation | Publication: ARCH o architektúre a inej kultúre, marec 2001

Das Tragwerk der Halle sieht in den Betonfundamenten eingespannte Stahlstützen vor, auf denen die 30 Meter weit überdeckenden Fischbauchträger aufsitzen. Ihre Konstruktion erfolgte großteils aus Massivholz, nur für die Untergurte wurde Brettschichtholz verwendet. Die Stege von variabler Höhe bestehen aus zwei Lagen gegenläufig diagonal verlaufender Bretter, die mit Obergurt und Untergurt verbunden sind. Die Fassadenelemente konnten weitgehend vorgefertigt werden, wobei im unteren Bereich die Stülpschalung mit Lüftungsspalten versehen wurde. Während nur vor der Südseite ein Vordach aus Brettstapelelementen an der Halle angefügt ist, zieht sich eine entsprechend abgehängte Platte beim offenen Dach allseitig um das gesamte Bauwerk, beschirmt den Randbereich und unterstützt den Eindruck von Leichtigkeit und Schweben.

The hall's load-bearing structure is based on steel struts fixed on cement foundations. It was completed with the 30 meter-high fish-bellied girders. These were mainly made of solid timber, although bonded timber panels were used on the bottom flanges. The vertically adjustable footbridges consist of two layers of diagonally placed timber boards that are connected to the top and bottom flanges. It was possible to prefabricate the larger part of the façade elements and the weather boarding was fitted with ventilation openings. Although only the south side features a canopy made of bonded timber elements, the corresponding suspended planking of the open roof wraps around the entire structure, covering the area at the edges and supporting the light, hovering impression.

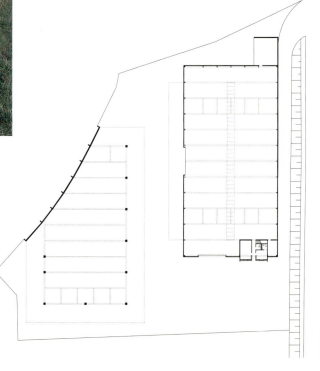

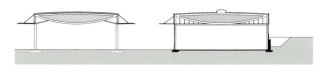

Hermann Kaufmann

Biomasseheizwerk, Lech

Biomass Energy Plant, Lech

Das große Gebäude, dessen Frontseite hoch aufragt, während das Dach pultartig flach nach hinten abfällt, liegt einige hundert Meter vor dem Dorf, vor einer Stelle, wo die Talflanken schluchtartig zusammenrücken und Straße und Flüsschen um die knappe Fläche wetteifern. Markant schafft es ein künstliches Engnis als Auftakt zum unmittelbar folgenden natürlichen Engnis. Es dialogisiert mit den Mitteln von Volumen, Proportion und Material mit der vorhandenen Situation und schafft zugleich einen neuen Ort. Als ökologisch wichtige Maßnahme zur Luftverbesserung im Kurort, wo bei den nicht seltenen Inversionslagen Hausbrand und Autoverkehr die Schadstoffkonzentration unangenehm ansteigen lassen, ist das Biomasseheizwerk Teil einer Basisinfrastruktur zur nachhaltigen Verbesserung des touristischen Angebots. Über diese Nutzfunktion hinaus bildet die äußere Hülle ein zeitgenössisches Element alpiner Baukunst. Wenn man darauf zufährt, fällt die Straße in einer Rechtskurve relativ steil ab. Ihrem äußeren Rand folgt konkav eine über zehn Meter hohe, oben mit Tannenholz verbretterte Wand. Der als Stützmauer niedrig beginnende, gestockte Betonsockel wird mit fallender Straße zunehmend höher, übernimmt dann die Funktion der Gebäudebasis, löst sich aber nach halber Länge auf in drei runde Stahlbetonstützen, hinter denen eine offene Vorhalle liegt. Hier befindet sich der Anlageteil. Immer höher wird die untere, nun verglaste Hälfte der Fassade, während die obere, holzverkleidete, dem Gefälle der Straße folgend, abnimmt. So interpretiert der Baukörper feinfühlig Topografie und Straßenverlauf. Die Stirnseiten sind leicht zurückgesetzt, an der Südseite in Form zweier gebäudehoher Schiebetore, so hoch, dass die Lastwagen zum Entladen der Hack- und Rindenschnitzel in die Speicher mit vorn hochgestemmtem Ladecontainer hinausschieben können. Geschlossen wirken sie eher abweisend, anders als die Nordfassade, deren Glaswand in der unteren Hälfte Einblick bietet und deren Vorhalle zu Besichtigungen einlädt.

The large building, with its high front façade and sharply declining flat roof pitch at the back, lies a few hundred meters from the village in a location where the flanks of the valley come together with the street and creek competing for the narrow expanse of space. The building's artificial narrowness provides an introduction for the natural narrowness following immediately afterwards. It generates dialogue by way of volume, proportions and materials while at the same time creating a new site. The construction of the biomass heating plant is one of the measures that were implemented to improve the air quality in the health resort area for tourism purposes. These measures were necessary due to the unpleasant increase in contaminating pollutants as a result of atmospheric inversions caused by house fires and traffic. Aside from these functional considerations, the exterior shell is also a sample of contemporary alpine architecture. When one drives towards it, the road drops off relatively steeply on a right curve. A ten-meter high wall trimmed with fir paneling at the top lines the outer edge of the road. The cement base course begins low as a supporting wall and becomes larger as the road drops off, assuming the function of the building's base, before dissolving into three round ferroconcrete struts, behind which lies an open anteroom where the housing project segment is located. The lower half of the façade, which features glass paneling in this segment begins to become larger here, while the upper, timber-clad half becomes smaller, following the road's terrain. Hence the building interprets both the topography and the road's trajectory with great feeling. The street-side fronts are slightly recessed, while the south side features two, building-high sliding gates to allow trucks to unload the minced meat and beef cutlet transports from their containers. They seem forbidding when closed as opposed to the north façade, which offers a view of the interior through the glass paneling on the bottom half and whose anteroom invites visitors to enter the building.

1999
Lech, Austria
Bauherrschaft | Client: Biomasse Heizwerk Lech GmbH & Co KG, Lech

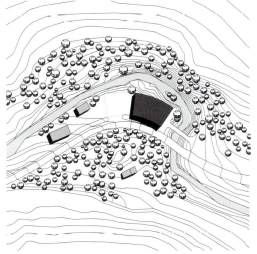

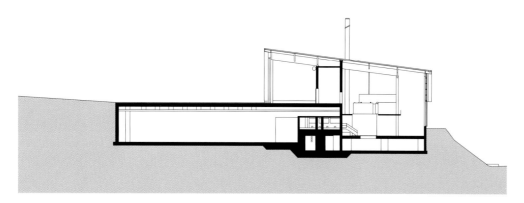

Schnitt
section

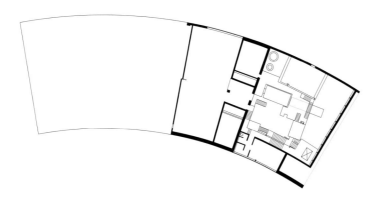

Obergeschoß
upper floor

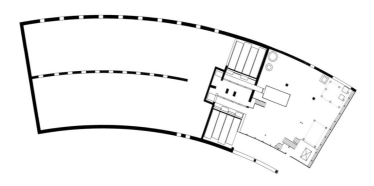

Erdgeschoß
ground floor

Hermann Kaufmann, Gerhard Aicher

Impulszentrum Bregenzerwald, Egg

Impulse Center Bregenzerwald, Egg

Auf dem ehemaligen Stationsgelände der schmalspurigen Bregenzerwaldbahn, das als künstlich vergrößerte Terrasse den südwestlich orientierten Hang unterbricht, galt es, zentrumbildende und den veränderten ökonomischen Bedürfnissen entsprechende Nutzungen zu platzieren. Der kompakte dreigeschoßige Baukörper nützt die Tiefe des Grundstücks und lässt an der Südost-, zugleich der Eingangsseite, ein Vorfeld offen für den in ländlichen Gegenden unabdingbaren Parkplatz. Die nordwestliche Hälfte des Grundstücks bleibt für künftige Entwicklungen frei. Das Grundrisskonzept sieht möglichst nutzungsneutrale Geschoßflächen vor, die um einen glasgedeckten Lichthof herum angeordnet sind. Ein massiver Kern mit Treppe, Aufzug und Sanitärräumen beschränkt sich auf einen kleinen Teil an der Nordostseite, die Geschoßflächen werden über Galerien erschlossen und sind mit Leichtbauwänden frei unterteilbar. Die wenigen Stützen stören dabei kaum. Der Haupteingang liegt axial an der Südostseite. Er wird von einem Café-Restaurant flankiert, dessen Terrasse um die Südecke herum die Sonnenstunden des Tages ausgiebig zu nutzen vermag. Der zentrale Lichthof weitet sich in Längsrichtung und mit zunehmender Geschoßzahl, sodass für unten Stehende kein Engegefühl aufkommt. Sein Natursteinboden wertet den Raum zusätzlich auf. Die schlanken, tragenden Schichtholzlamellen unter dem Glasdach bieten einen lokalen Materialbezug mit zeitgenössischer Holztechnologie und verweisen auf das aktuelle Leistungspotenzial der Zimmerleute aus dem Bregenzerwald. In dem durchaus sparsam errichteten Gebäude erhalten die wenigen gestalterischen Elemente zusammen mit den klaren Proportionen ein ähnliches Gesicht wie der klassische Aufbau und ein Fensterornament an einer Scheune, dem bäuerlichen Ökonomiegebäude, oder an einer vielachsig befensterten Fabrik aus dem 19. Jahrhundert. Damit bewegt sich der Neubau mit zeitgenössischen Formen in einer selbstverständlichen Tradition vergleichbarer größerer Bauvolumen dieser Gegend.

The objective on the former "Bregenzerwaldbahn" narrow-gauge train station grounds, with the artificially expanded terrace that interrupts the southwest oriented slope, was to create a center that kept up with changing economic needs. The compact three-level building uses the depth of the plot by leaving the southeastern side, which is also the entrance, open for the parking lot that is always required in rural projects. The northwestern half of the site was left vacant for future development. The grounds plan was designed to create multi-purpose levels that are aligned around a glass-ceilinged inner court. A solid core with stairs, an elevator and sanitary facilities is located in a small segment of the building on the northeastern side. Access to the levels is possible via galleries that can be partitioned individually with lightweight separating panels. The low amount of struts employed in the structure is hardly an obstacle. The main entrance is located axially along the southeastern side. It is flanked by a café-restaurant with a terrace on the south corner that takes in hours of sun throughout the day. The central inner court extends longitudinally and in correspondence to the increasing number of stories. This allows visitors standing below to feel unconstricted. The natural stone floor enhances the room's effect. The slender, the laminated timber load-bearing slats under the glass roof are made of materials available in the region in combination with contemporary structural timber technology and display the current potential of the area's carpenters. In the very reduced building, the few design elements combine with the clear proportions to create a likeness similar to the classical structure and window ornamentation of a barn, a farming facility or to a 19th century factory with its windows at many axes. Hence the new annex's contemporary shape is in accordance with the natural tradition of comparable, larger buildings in the area.

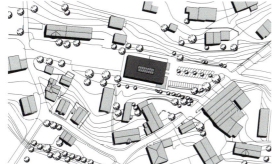

2000
Egg, Austria
Bauherrschaft | Client: Raiffeisenbank Mittelbregenzerwald, Egg
Mitarbeit | Assistence: Christoph Dünser, Harald Seidler, Norbert Kaufmann

80 Industrie- und Gewerbebauten · Industrial and Commercial Buildings

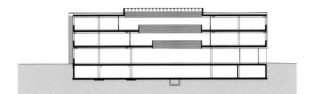

Längsschnitt
longitudinal section

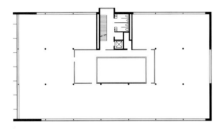

1. und 2. Obergeschoß
first and second floor

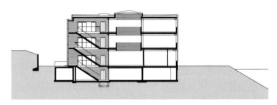

Querschnitt
cross section

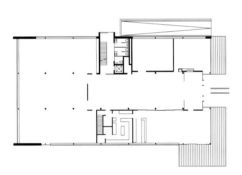

Erdgeschoß
ground floor

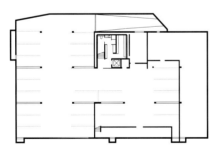

Untergeschoß
basement

0　10　20 m

Industrie- und Gewerbebauten　　　Industrial and Commercial Buildings

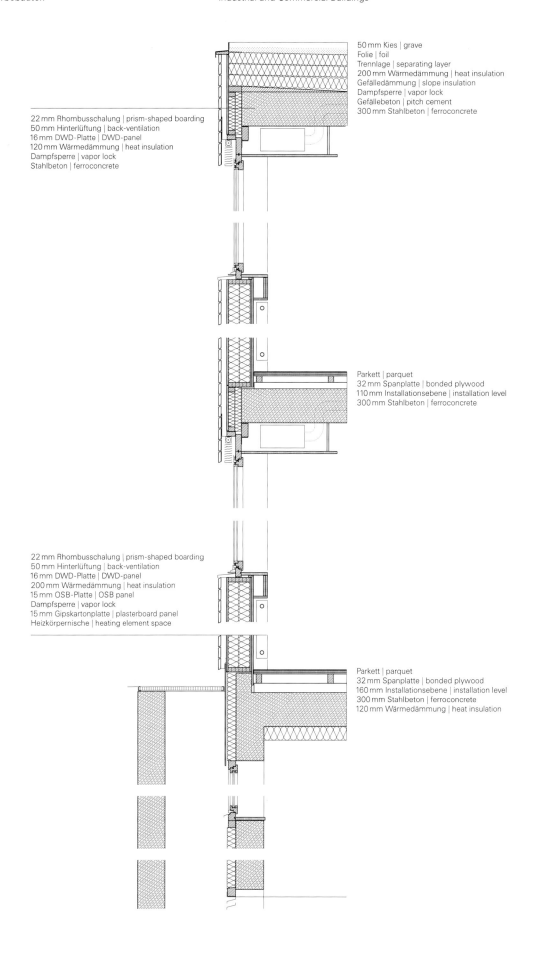

22 mm Rhombusschalung | prism-shaped boarding
50 mm Hinterlüftung | back-ventilation
16 mm DWD-Platte | DWD-panel
120 mm Wärmedämmung | heat insulation
Dampfsperre | vapor lock
Stahlbeton | ferroconcrete

50 mm Kies | grave
Folie | foil
Trennlage | separating layer
200 mm Wärmedämmung | heat insulation
Gefälledämmung | slope insulation
Dampfsperre | vapor lock
Gefällebeton | pitch cement
300 mm Stahlbeton | ferroconcrete

Parkett | parquet
32 mm Spanplatte | bonded plywood
110 mm Installationsebene | installation level
300 mm Stahlbeton | ferroconcrete

22 mm Rhombusschalung | prism-shaped boarding
50 mm Hinterlüftung | back-ventilation
16 mm DWD-Platte | DWD-panel
200 mm Wärmedämmung | heat insulation
15 mm OSB-Platte | OSB panel
Dampfsperre | vapor lock
15 mm Gipskartonplatte | plasterboard panel
Heizkörpernische | heating element space

Parkett | parquet
32 mm Spanplatte | bonded plywood
160 mm Installationsebene | installation level
300 mm Stahlbeton | ferroconcrete
120 mm Wärmedämmung | heat insulation

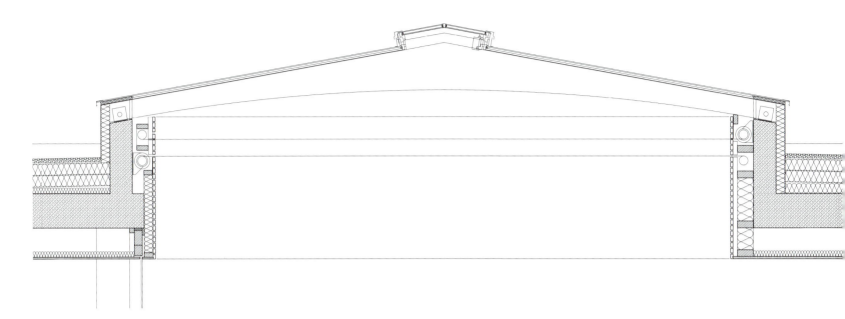

Der Stahlbetonskelettbau mit einer aussteifenden Scheibe und dem massiven Kern ist mit vorgefertigten, wärmegedämmten Brüstungselementen aus Holzwerkstoffen und mit Holz-Alufenstern klimadicht gemacht. Als Wetterschutz dient eine hinterlüftete Rhombusschalung aus Tanne, deren Bretter mit Lüftungsfugen versetzt sind, damit sie rasch trocknen. Auf ein Vordach wurde bewusst verzichtet, damit die Abwitterung der Fassade gleichmäßig erfolgt. Das Glasdach über dem Lichthof wird mit einer Schar Brettschichtträger überspannt. Sie sind zur Mitte überhöht sodass ein flacher Grat entsteht. Direktes Sonnenlicht wird mit ausrollbaren Stoffbahnen abgehalten. Bei Wärmestau öffnen sich Lüftungsklappen. Das Zusammenspiel der als Speicher dienenden, sichtbar belassenen Betondecken, der Gebäudelüftung mit Erdkollektor und einer optimalen Wärmedämmung ergibt ein gutes Sommerklima, das eine technische Kühlung überflüssig macht.

The ferroconcrete skeleton structure, including its stiffening disk and solid core, was equipped with prefabricated insulated balustrade timber components and wood-aluminum composite windows for protection against the elements. Back-ventilated, helm-shaped pine wood revetments, whose panels have ventilation openings for quick drying, are used for protection against the weather. The building has no canopy to allow the façade to weather evenly. A set of bonded timber struts was spread across the glass-ceiling inner court section. They are elevated in the middle, creating a flat grid. Direct sunlight is deflected with rolling cloth panels. Vents open to counter overheating. The interplay of the unfinished cement roof which stores heat, and the building's ventilation system featuring a energy collector and ideal insulation, result in pleasant summer temperatures that make a technical cooling solution superfluous.

Hermann Kaufmann, Christian Lenz

Architekturbüro, Schwarzach

Architecture Office, Schwarzach

Der lang gezogene Baukörper befindet sich am nördlichen Dorfrand, wo die Bebauung übergeht in Sportanlagen und Baumgärten und schon bald der Siedlungsrand des benachbarten Dorfes beginnt. Die Bauhöhe stimmt mit den nahen Ein- und Zweifamilienhäusern überein, mit seiner Länge gewinnt der aufgestelzte Quader jedoch siedlungsbauliche Zeichenhaftigkeit und markiert in der Baustruktur eine Kante, auch wenn noch zwei, drei Häuser davor zu stehen kommen sollten. Das Erdgeschoß wird durchgehend von Büroflächen eingenommen, wovon einige individuelle Kojen und Besprechungsräume akustisch und optisch abgetrennt sind. Zur Verbesserung der Raumakustik hängen unter der glatten Sichtbetondecke den Schall absorbierende Elemente aus Heraklith. Als Boden dienen lackierte Spanplatten. Das Obergeschoß enthält vier Wohnungen, die nach Süden auf eine vorgelagerte Terrasse hin organisiert sind. Es kragt an beiden Längsseiten vor, beschirmt die Bürofenster und bietet nordseitig einen regengeschützten Weg zu den parkierten Autos. Zwei einfache Holztreppen sind hier frei an den Hauptbaukörper dazugestellt. Gegen Schlagregen schützt sie ein dunkles Kunststoffgewebe. Die Obergeschoßfassaden sind mit Douglastanne-Sperrholz beplankt. Wie dieses stammen einige Materialien im Verschleißbereich aus dem unteren Kostensegment, weil die Entwerfer den Prozess ihrer Alterung mitverfolgen wollen, ein Experiment, das man einem anderen Bauherrn selbstverständlich nicht zumuten möchte. Die individuell gestalteten Wohnungen sind räumlich großzügig und funktional kompakt organisiert. Schmalhohe Brettschichtträger unter der Decke geben dem einen Wohnraum ein attraktives Gepräge und wirken raumakustisch günstig. Eine klare architektonische Struktur, funktionale Büroräume und ein ansprechender Wohnwert im Obergeschoß verbinden sich an diesem Bau mit undogmatischer Pragmatik und zeitgemäßer Sparsamkeit in Fragen des Energieverbrauchs zu einem kostengünstigen Musterbau als Beleg für Erfahrung und Leistungsfähigkeit des gemeinsamen Architekturbüros.

The elongated structure is located on the northern edge of the village, where the developed area continues with sports facilities and tree schools before reaching the edge of the neighboring village's developed areas. The building height is in keeping with that of the single-family units in the vicinity, but the stilts under the square-shaped structure give it additional relief and help create an edge, even if two or three buildings are added to the site. The entire ground floor is occupied by office spaces, some of which are divided into individual, acoustically and visually separate carrels and meeting rooms. Heraklith sound damping elements hanging from the smooth, unfinished cement ceiling are designed to improve the room's acoustics. Lacquered chipboard panels were used for the floors. The upper level contains four apartments that are aligned facing south on a projecting terrace. The terrace projects forward on the longitudinal sides, protecting the office windows and features a walkway offering protection from the rain on the way to the cars parked on the premises. Two simple timber staircases were added to the main structure here. A dark synthetic fabric protects visitors from rainbursts. The façade of the upper level is covered with Douglas fir plywood cladding. This and other materials used on wearing sections of the building are low cost items chosen by the designers in order to track their aging process. However, of course this experiment could not be borne by the contractors. The individually designed apartments are generous in terms of space and their organization is both functional and compact. Slender, high timber struts under the roof have a favorable effect on the room's acoustics. A clear architectural structure, functional office spaces and an appealing quality of life on the upper level are all achieved in this building with undogmatic pragmatism and a contemporary sense of cost-consciousness in terms of energy consumption. This makes the building a low-cost sample of the joint architecture office's acumen and experience.

1999
Schwarzach, Austria
Bauherrschaft | Client: Miterrichtergemeinschaft Lenz/Kaufmann/Gmeiner, Schwarzach; Revital Bauträger GmbH, Dornbirn
Mitarbeit | Assistence: Peter Nussbaumer, Wolfgang Elmenreich
Publikation | Publication: Architektur & Technik, 12/2001

Industrie- und Gewerbebauten Industrial and Commercial Buildings

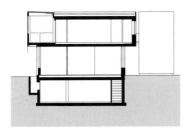

Querschnitt
cross section

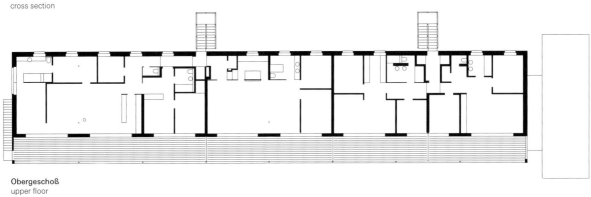

Obergeschoß
upper floor

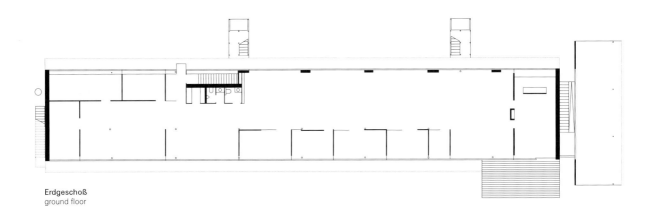

Erdgeschoß
ground floor

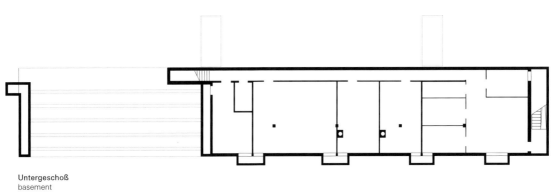

Untergeschoß
basement

0   5   10 m

Das Ausführungskonzept kombiniert verschiedene Materialien nach ihrer konstruktiven, ökonomischen und bauphysikalischen Sinnhaftigkeit. Der Keller, die aussteifenden Mauerscheiben im Erdgeschoß und die Decke zwischen Erd- und Obergeschoß wurden in Ortbeton errichtet. Sie dienen als Speichermasse und dem Schallschutz. Die Decke über dem Keller, das Dach und die Außenwände sind hingegen als gedämmte Hohlkastenkonstruktionen vorgefertigt, während für die Innenstützen schlanke Stahlrohre Verwendung fanden. Im Bürobereich konnte unter Verwendung einfacher Standardträger für den Schalungsbau ein Hohlboden für Installationen vorgesehen werden, während in den Wohnungen schlanke Brettschichtbalken aus Douglasie zwischen die primären Stahlträger gelegt sind. Die hochwertig wärmegedämmten Außenwände sind als vorgefertigte, beidseitig mit Holzspanplatten gedeckte Kastenkonstruktionen ausgeführt. Der gesamte Materialeinsatz erfolgt erfrischend undogmatisch und ohne moralisierenden Unterton.

The execution of the building combines different materials according to their purpose in terms of construction, economic and structural properties. The cellar, the stiffening wall panels on the ground floor and the ceiling between the ground and upper level all serve as heat storing surfaces and provide acoustic damping. Whereas the ceiling over the cellar, the roof and the exterior walls are all prefabricated insulated box structures. Slender steel struts were used in the interior for support. The use of simple standard girders made it possible to create a hollow floor in the panel structure for installations, while the apartments feature slender Douglas fir timber struts between the primary steel stays. The high quality insulating exterior walls are prefabricated box-shaped elements featuring bonded timber cladding on both sides. All the materials used are refreshingly undogmatic and devoid of a moralizing undertone.

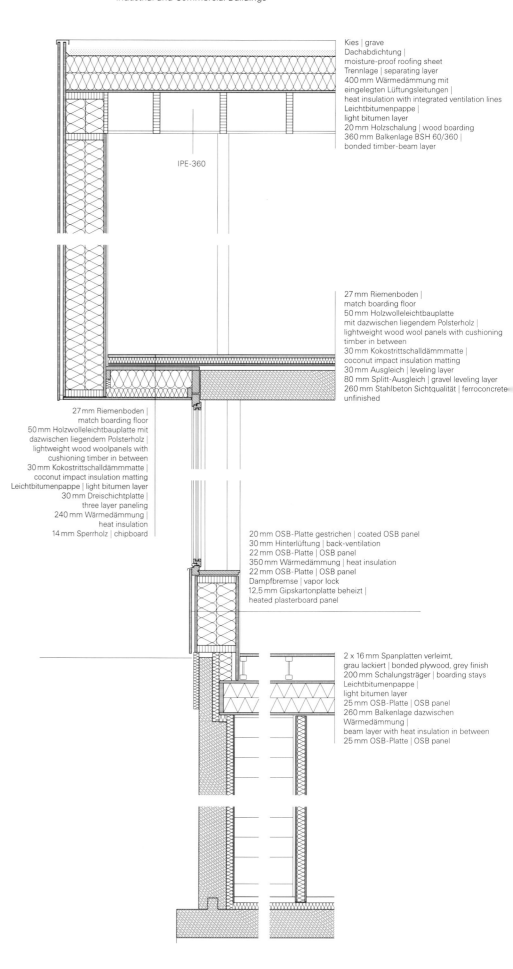

Kies | grave
Dachabdichtung | moisture-proof roofing sheet
Trennlage | separating layer
400 mm Wärmedämmung mit eingelegten Lüftungsleitungen | heat insulation with integrated ventilation lines
Leichtbitumenpappe | light bitumen layer
20 mm Holzschalung | wood boarding
360 mm Balkenlage BSH 60/360 | bonded timber-beam layer

IPE-360

27 mm Riemenboden | match boarding floor
50 mm Holzwolleleichtbauplatte mit dazwischen liegendem Polsterholz | lightweight wood wool panels with cushioning timber in between
30 mm Kokostrittschalldämmmatte | coconut impact insulation matting
30 mm Ausgleich | leveling layer
80 mm Splitt-Ausgleich | gravel leveling layer
260 mm Stahlbeton Sichtqualität | ferroconcrete unfinished

27 mm Riemenboden | match boarding floor
50 mm Holzwolleleichtbauplatte mit dazwischen liegendem Polsterholz | lightweight wood woolpanels with cushioning timber in between
30 mm Kokostrittschalldämmmatte | coconut impact insulation matting
Leichtbitumenpappe | light bitumen layer
30 mm Dreischichtplatte | three layer paneling
240 mm Wärmedämmung | heat insulation
14 mm Sperrholz | chipboard

20 mm OSB-Platte gestrichen | coated OSB panel
30 mm Hinterlüftung | back-ventilation
22 mm OSB-Platte | OSB panel
350 mm Wärmedämmung | heat insulation
22 mm OSB-Platte | OSB panel
Dampfbremse | vapor lock
12,5 mm Gipskartonplatte beheizt | heated plasterboard panel

2 x 16 mm Spanplatten verleimt, grau lackiert | bonded plywood, grey finish
200 mm Schalungsträger | boarding stays
Leichtbitumenpappe | light bitumen layer
25 mm OSB-Platte | OSB panel
260 mm Balkenlage dazwischen Wärmedämmung | beam layer with heat insulation in between
25 mm OSB-Platte | OSB panel

Christian Lenz

Zahnambulatorium VGKK, Bregenz
VGKK Dentistry Clinic, Bregenz

Das winkelförmige Bauwerk befindet sich in flachem Gelände, wo westlich des Stadtkerns das Delta der Bregenzer Ach beginnt. Das Quartier zwischen Bundesstraße und Bahnlinie, die es in großem Bogen einfasst, weist eine gemischte Bebauung auf. Einzelne vorstädtische Nachbarhäuser stammen noch aus der ersten Hälfte des 20. Jahrhunderts, einige Vielgeschoßer aus Boomzeiten der zweiten Hälfte. Der breit gelagerte dreigeschoßige Neubau weist parallel zur Straße einen langen Gebäudeflügel auf, während mit dem kürzeren Trakt die Tiefe des dreieckigen Grundstücks genützt wird. Der offene Raumwinkel fasst im Norden einen Gartenhof, den ein Hain Kirschbäume füllt. Die Fassaden sind mit großen Scheiben geschoßhoch verglast, schlanke Fensterprofile durchschneiden die membranartigen Flächen, die rhythmisch unterbrochen werden von schmalhohen Lüftungsflügeln in Lärchenholzrahmen. Die feine Zeichnung der Fassade lässt das Bauwerk freundlich und durchlässig wirken. Vor harter Sonneneinstrahlung schützen außen liegende Rafflamellen. Die beiden Traktstirnen und eine Eckfläche zum Nachbarhaus sind mit Sichtbetonscheiben geschlossen. Die perfekte Glätte der Zementhaut nimmt dem Material die rohe Härte, sodass Glas und Beton keinen Gegensatz bilden, sondern gemeinsam einen sorgfältig-eleganten, ja geradezu edlen Eindruck erwecken. Das Innere entspricht mit dem dunklen Natursteinboden in der weiträumigen Empfangshalle dem von außen gewonnenen Bild. Ein verglaster Lift und eine spannungsvoll um die tragende Betonscheibe herum entwickelte Treppenanlage leiten hinauf ins erste Obergeschoß, wo ein bequem möbliertes, lang gezogenes Foyer das Warten vor den Behandlungszimmern erleichtert. Das gesamte Bauwerk erscheint freundlich, und im Zusammenwirken mit der Inneneinrichtung aus ansprechend gestalteten Holzmöbeln wird die Absicht deutlich, einer nicht unbedingt angenehmen Behandlung ein positives Raum- und Architekturklima zu unterlegen. Dies gelingt mit subtiler Eleganz und und einer konsequenten Liebe zum zurückhaltend gestalteten Detail.

The angular building is located on a flat plot of land to the west of the center of the city, where the Bregenzer Ach delta begins. The large curving area between the interstate road and the railway lines is defined by mixed forms of development. Individual neighboring suburban houses in the vicinity were built in the first half of the 20th century, while some of the four-story buildings were built during the boom period of the second half of the last century. The widely set, new three-story building features a long wing set parellel to the road, while the shorter wing makes use of the triangular site's depth. The corner of open space to the north comprises a garden with a cherry tree grove. The walls defining the length of the building feature floor-to-ceiling glass paneling, while narrow window profiles cut into the membrane-like surfaces. These surfaces are inerrupted with rythmically placed, slender and tall ventilation vents with larch wood frames. The fine drafting of the façade gives the building a friendly and permeable appearance. Sliding slats mounted on the outside protect the building from harsh sunlight. The two gable ends of the wings and a corner surface facing the neighboring house are closed with slabs of unfinished cement. The perfect smoothness of the cement skin takes the edge off the material's raw hardness, hence glass and cement are not juxtaposed here. Instead, they create a carefully elegant, almost refined impression. The interiors, with the dark natural stone floor of the reception area emphasize the impression created outside. A glass elevator and a staircase wrapped excitingly around the supporting cement disk take the visitor up to a comfortably furnished foyer that helps shorten waiting times on the first upper level in front of the treatment rooms. The entire building seems friendly and the interplay between the interiors with the appealingly designed wooden furniture make the intention clear of giving spaces for treatments that aren't necessarily pleasant a positive room and architectural climate. This attempt succeded with subtle elegance and loving attention to the use of restrained design.

2001
Bregenz, Austria
Bauherrschaft | Client: Vorarlberger Gebietskrankenkasse, Dornbirn
Statik | Structural engineering: Christian Gantner, Nenzing
Mitarbeit | Assistence: Jürgen Erath, Edda Lohmann
Kunst am Bau | Artwork: Karl Heinz Ströhle
Gartenarchitektin | Landscape Architect: Barbara Bacher

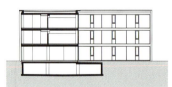

Querschnitt / Ansicht
cross section / elevation

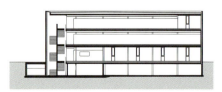

Längsschnitt
longitudinal section

93 Industrie- und Gewerbebauten　　　Industrial and Commercial Buildings

2. Obergeschoß
second floor

1. Obergeschoß
first floor

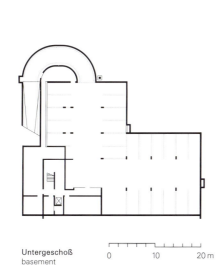

Untergeschoß
basement

0　10　20 m

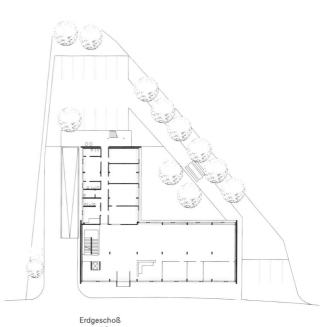

Erdgeschoß
ground floor

Christian Lenz

Spenglerei Rusch, Alberschwende

Rusch Plumbing, Alberschwende

Der Gewerbebetrieb befindet sich östlich des Dorfkerns, unterhalb der Straße auf einem leicht nach Norden abfallenden Hang. Im Osten rauscht am Grundstück ein Bach vorbei. Man fährt von Süden zu und erreicht einen trapezförmigen, platzartigen Hof vor der Werkhalle, der an der gegenüberliegenden Seite von einem Garagentrakt begrenzt wird. Nach Westen schließt an die Werkhalle ein Büroteil an, er ist zweigeschoßig und weist eine Glasfassade auf, deren Fächer teils verglast, teils mit Sandwichelementen ausgefacht sind. Das Muster von geschlossen oder offen erscheint zufällig und nimmt auch nicht Bezug auf die Geschoßteilung. Diese gestalterische Maßnahme erschwert auf Distanz eine Fixierung der Größenordnung. Der Baukörper wirkt somit als ein ungegliedertes Ganzes, das heißt auch monumentaler, mithin im landschaftlichen Kontext prominenter. Bekleidet ist er mit einer Textur, die erzeugt wird aus dem Gitter der Fenstersprossen und der freien Verteilung von Gläsern und Paneelen. Das Kupferblech, mit dem letztere außen geschützt sind, belegt die handwerkliche Leistungsfähigkeit des Betriebs. Der Innenausbau der Stahlskelettkonstruktion zeigt dagegen viel Holz: Decken aus gehobelten, sichtbar belassenen Brettstapelplatten, Sperrholzverkleidungen an den Fassadenpaneelen und Stäbchenparkett am Boden. Auch die Werkhalle wird von Trägern aus Brettschichtholz überspannt, und für das auskragende Vordach sowie den Wetterschirm, die sich zu einem schlanken Rahmen verbinden, kamen wieder Brettstapelplatten zur Anwendung, die auf der bewitterten Seite eine Blechverkleidung tragen. Die Fassadenverkleidung der Halle besteht wieder aus Metall, diesmal ist es Zinkblech. Die architektonische Gestaltung des Gewerbebauwerks und dessen Ausführung zeugen von Sorgfalt und Genauigkeit; Tugenden, die einen guten Handwerksbetrieb auszeichnen. Als effektiver Werbeträger darf das Bauwerk daher nicht bloß aus der Ferne attraktiv wirken, sondern muss auch von nahe besehen Stand halten und auf dem ureigensten Gebiet der Branche, jenem handwerklicher Qualität in der Ausführung, Vertrauen erwecken.

The business enterprise is located to the east of the village center, under the road of a slope that drops of gently to the north. A creek rushes past the plot to the east. The site can be accessed from the south and it features a trapezoid-shaped forecourt-like square in front of the production hall, which is bordered by a garage wing acorss the way. To the west, the production hall includes a two-story office area with a glass façade whose webbing is partly glass-paneled and partly completed with sandwich components. The open or closed pattern seems coincidental and does not correspond to the floor division. This design measure makes it difficult to gauge the structure's size from the distance. Hence the building seems to be an organzed unit. This also means it apears more monumental and more prominent within the rural context. It is clad with a texture that is created by the gratings of the window mullions and the free distribution glass and paneling. The copper plating bears testament to the company's acumen in its field of expertise. On the other hand, the interior of the steel skeleton structure features large amounts of timber components: The ceilings are made of planed, unfinished bonded timber panels. Other elements include the plywood cladding on the façade panels and the parquet strip floors. The production hall also features bonded timber stays and bonded timber panels were used on the linked projecting canopy and weather screen. These components support a layer of sheet metal cladding on the side exposed to the elements. The hall's façade paneling is made of tin sheet metal. The architectural design of the industrial facility and its execution are proof of careful work and precision, two qualities that distinguish good craftsmanship. As an effective advertising vehicle, the building has to be appealing both at a distance and up close and instill confidence in the company's most important strength, which is the quality of its craftmanship.

2002
Alberschwende, Austria
Bauherrschaft | Client: Gunther Rusch GesmbH, Alberschwende
Mitarbeit | Assistence: Helmut Brunner

Industrie- und Gewerbebauten   Industrial and Commercial Buildings

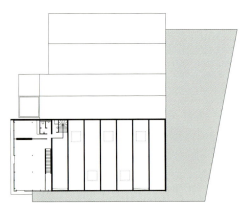

Obergeschoß
upper floor

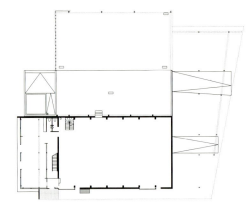

Erdgeschoß
ground floor

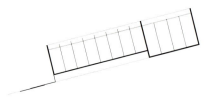

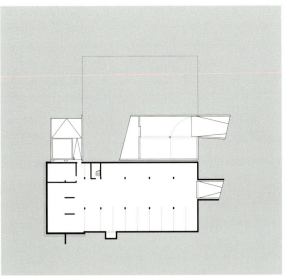

Untergeschoß
basement

99 Industrie- und Gewerbebauten   Industrial and Commercial Buildings

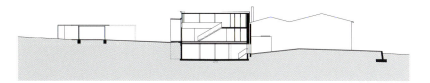

Querschnitt
cross section

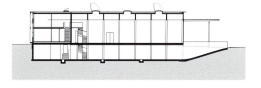

Längsschnitt
longitudinal section

Das Tragwerk des Büroteils ist aus Stahlprofilen aufgebaut, die Decken bestehen aus Brettstapelplatten, die in die Profile eingeschoben wurden, und das Untergeschoß ist in Ortbeton ausgeführt. Die Glasfassade verfügt über ein statisches System aus schlanken, horizontal geführten Brettschichtträgern, die gegen den Winddruck an den Stahlstützen anliegen. Die Steher hinter den vertikalen Sprossen sind dazwischen gesetzt. Für eine Fassade dieser eher geringen Ausdehnung erlaubt eine Substruktion aus Holz im Zusammenwirken mit dem Stahltragwerk erstaunlich schlanke Dimensionen und elegante Proportionen. Die ausklappbaren Lüftungsflügel sind als Rahmenkonstruktion ebenfalls aus Holz ausgeführt. Die Fassade, die einer reinen Metall-Glaskonstruktion architektonisch und bauphysikalisch in nichts nachsteht, konnte von den regionalen Handwerkern gefertigt werden und zeugt von einem hohen technischen Niveau. Als Sonnenschutz dienen Stoffstores, die vor der Westfassade heruntergezogen werden können.

The supporting structure consists partly of steel beams. The ceilings are made of bonded timber panels that were inserted in the beams and the lower level was built using local cement. The structural system of the slender, horizontally set bonded timber struts that rest on the steel beams for support against the wind. The stays behind the vertical steps are located in between. The rather modest size of the façade made it possible to use a timber sub-structure along with the steel support system façade. This lead to astonishingly slim dimensions and proportions. The frames of collapsing ventilation slats are also timber components. The façade, which is not inferior to a pure metal and glass structure in structural terms in any way, was made by craftsmen in the region.

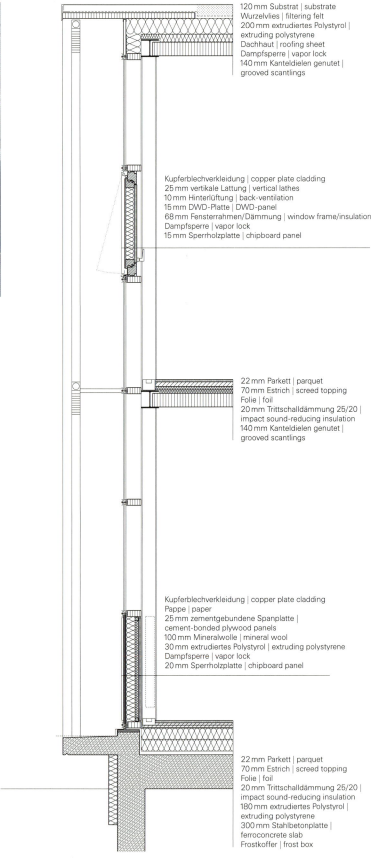

120 mm Substrat | substrate
Wurzelvlies | filtering felt
200 mm extrudiertes Polystyrol | extruding polystyrene
Dachhaut | roofing sheet
Dampfsperre | vapor lock
140 mm Kanteldielen genutet | grooved scantlings

Kupferblechverkleidung | copper plate cladding
25 mm vertikale Lattung | vertical lathes
10 mm Hinterlüftung | back-ventilation
15 mm DWD-Platte | DWD-panel
68 mm Fensterrahmen/Dämmung | window frame/insulation
Dampfsperre | vapor lock
15 mm Sperrholzplatte | chipboard panel

22 mm Parkett | parquet
70 mm Estrich | screed topping
Folie | foil
20 mm Trittschalldämmung 25/20 | impact sound-reducing insulation
140 mm Kanteldielen genutet | grooved scantlings

Kupferblechverkleidung | copper plate cladding
Pappe | paper
25 mm zementgebundene Spanplatte | cement-bonded plywood panels
100 mm Mineralwolle | mineral wool
30 mm extrudiertes Polystyrol | extruding polystyrene
Dampfsperre | vapor lock
20 mm Sperrholzplatte | chipboard panel

22 mm Parkett | parquet
70 mm Estrich | screed topping
Folie | foil
20 mm Trittschalldämmung 25/20 | impact sound-reducing insulation
180 mm extrudiertes Polystyrol | extruding polystyrene
300 mm Stahlbetonplatte | ferroconcrete slab
Frostkoffer | frost box

Christian Lenz

Aufstockung Ivoclar, Schaan, Liechtenstein

Ivoclar Expansion, Schaan, Liechtenstein

Im Dreieck zwischen den Bahngeleisen und der nordwärts nach Bendern führenden Straße stehen zahlreiche Industriebauten von teils riesigen Ausmaßen. In Ermangelung anderer Entwicklungsflächen musste der Ausbau von Produktions- und Büroräumen in Form einer Aufstockung auf die bestehende Fabrik vorgesehen werden. Der Entwurf legte ein zusätzliches aus Stahl und Holz konstruiertes Geschoß auf den mit Profilblech verkleideten alten Betonelementbau. Die wegen der Lastverteilung erforderliche Unterkonstruktion erzwang einen Zwischenraum, der aus einiger Entfernung als überdimensionale Schattennut in Erscheinung tritt. Das umlaufende Bandfenster des Neubauteils wird von den zwei kupferoxidgrünen Streifen der Brüstung und des Dachabschlusses eingefasst, sodass eine eigenständige Großform entsteht, die das lange Gebäude klar nach oben abschließt. Eine Verkleidung des vorhandenen Technikturms mit dem gleichen oxidierten Kupferblech ordnet dieses vertikale Element optisch dem Neubau zu. Horizontale und Vertikale bilden damit ein auf Fernwirkung bedachtes Zeichen. Zugleich wird das abgesetzte oberste Geschoß über den Turm optisch am Boden verankert und damit seine ebenfalls optische Tendenz zu horizontalem Wegdriften entschieden gebremst. Es sind dies einfache gestalterische Maßnahmen, die allerdings effizient sind, weil sie einem tektonischen Konzept folgen und die Anmutung insgesamt verbessern, ohne dass der Altbestand, der normalen Industriestandards entspricht, in seiner Erscheinung herabgesetzt wird. Im Innern dienen über zwei Drittel der Neubaufläche der Produktion. Im verbleibenden Rest sind Büros und Besprechungsräume angeordnet. Ein kleines Atrium holt von oben Licht in den Foyerbereich, der damit aufgewertet wird und in dem rational ökonomischen Kontext auch im Inneren für zeitgenössische Architekturqualität ein Merkzeichen setzt.

A number of industrial buildings lie in the triangle between the railroad tracks and the road leading to Bendern to the north, some of which are enormous. The expansion of the existing production and office spaces was limited to the premises of the existing factory due to a lack of other other development possibilities. The design set an additional steel-timber level on the profiled tin roof of the old cement component building. The substructure required for strain distribution purposes made it necessary to leave a gap between the old and new structures. From the distance, this space appears to be an overdimensional, shadowy groove in the building. The ribbon of windows set along the sides of the new level are framed by the two oxidized copper green stripes of the balustrade and the roof stop creating a unique large shape that clearly defines the long building's height. The oxidized copper green cladding of the technical tower links this vertical element with the new structure visually. Hence the horizontal and vertical aspects of the project create a symbol calculated for maximum effect when viewed form the distance. At the same time, the uppermost level above the tower is visually related to the ground, thereby minimizing its tendency to seemingly drift away visually from the structure horizontally. These simple design elements are also efficient since they follow a tectonic concept and improve the overall impression of the building without upstaging the old existing building, which was built according to normal industrial standards. Over two thirds of the newly constructed surface is sed for production purposes. The remaining space is occupied by offices and meeting rooms. A small atrium brings light to the foyer area from above, which enhances the area and also serves as a reminder of the quality of contemporary architecture within a rational-economic context.

2002
Schaan, Liechtenstein
Bauherrschaft | Client: Ivoclar-Vivadent AG, Schaan/FL
Statik | Structural engineering: Merz Kaufmann Partner GmbH, Dornbirn
Mitarbeit | Assistence: Gerhard Matt

Industrie- und Gewerbebauten — Industrial and Commercial Buildings

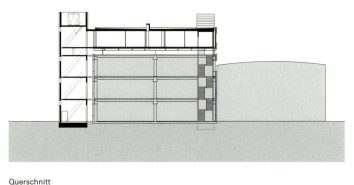

Querschnitt
cross section

0   10   20 m

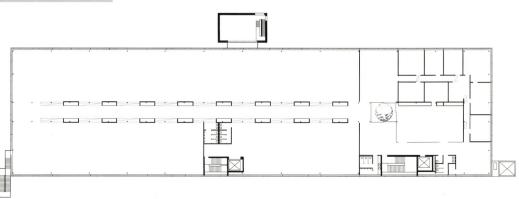

Grundriss
floor plan

Industrie- und Gewerbebauten — Industrial and Commercial Buildings

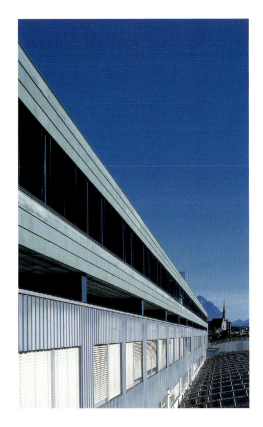

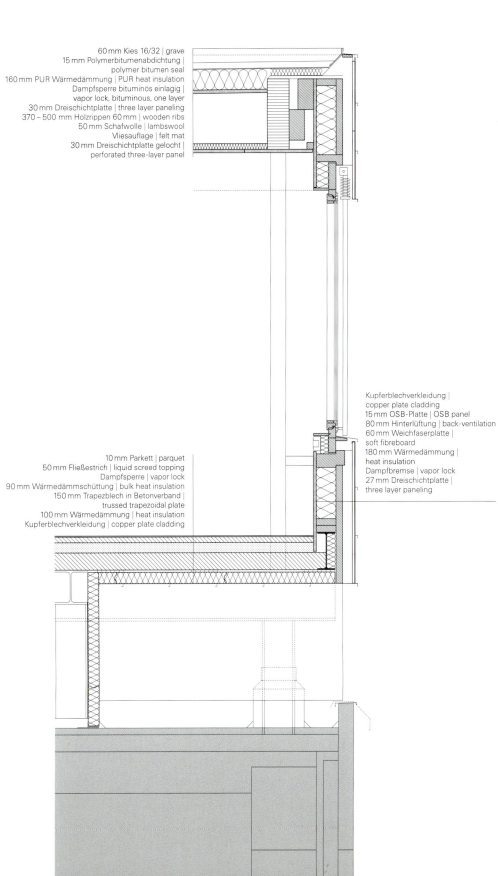

60 mm Kies 16/32 | grave
15 mm Polymerbitumenabdichtung | polymer bitumen seal
160 mm PUR Wärmedämmung | PUR heat insulation
Dampfsperre bituminös einlagig | vapor lock, bituminous, one layer
30 mm Dreischichtplatte | three layer paneling
370–500 mm Holzrippen 60 mm | wooden ribs
50 mm Schafwolle | lambswool
Vliesauflage | felt mat
30 mm Dreischichtplatte gelocht | perforated three-layer panel

Kupferblechverkleidung | copper plate cladding
15 mm OSB-Platte | OSB panel
80 mm Hinterlüftung | back-ventilation
60 mm Weichfaserplatte | soft fibreboard
180 mm Wärmedämmung | heat insulation
Dampfbremse | vapor lock
27 mm Dreischichtplatte | three layer paneling

10 mm Parkett | parquet
50 mm Fließestrich | liquid screed topping
Dampfsperre | vapor lock
90 mm Wärmedämmschüttung | bulk heat insulation
150 mm Trapezblech in Betonverband | trussed trapezoidal plate
100 mm Wärmedämmung | heat insulation
Kupferblechverkleidung | copper plate cladding

Christian Lenz

Büro- und Geschäftshaus MONO, Dornbirn
MONO Office and Commercial Building, Dornbirn

Der zweigeschoßige, über dem leicht eingezogenen Erdgeschoß aufgestelzte Quader steht an der Verbindungsstrecke von Dornbirn nach Lustenau, die zugleich den Anschluss an die Autobahn bildet. An dieser Straße reihen sich jene typischen, im ausgehenden 20. Jahrhundert schnell errichteten Verkaufshallen für Autos, Möbel, Kleider usw., die diesen Einfallsstraßen ihren spezifischen Charakter postmoderner, automobilgestützter Urbanität mitgeben. In der Menge marktschreierischer Signale und Symbole, mit denen die Umgebung überschwemmt wird, wirken die einfache Form des Baukörpers und der dunkelgraue Verputz angenehm ruhig. Das verglaste Erdgeschoß entspricht heutigen Bedürfnissen nach Einblick in den Verkaufsbereich. Die geschlossene Stirnseite der Obergeschoße, die zur Straße wie ein großes leeres Paneel erscheint, gibt schweigend ihren Kommentar zum Umfeld ab. An den Seitenfassaden sind breite, elegant proportionierte Fenster angeordnet, die jedoch den Vorrang der Mauerfläche nicht in Frage stellen. So bleibt der körperhafte Charakter des Gebäudes gewahrt. Das Besondere daran ist die Art und Weise, wie es unspektakulär ist und doch erinnerbar bleibt. Dies gelingt mit den sorgfältig abgewogenen Verhältnissen der Öffnungen zur geschlossenen Mauer sowie mit der Wirkung des aufgestelzten Körpers als einem Ganzen, das von keiner Unregelmäßigkeit gestört wird. Das Innere des Gebäudes ist dagegen geprägt von radikaler Ökonomie und nutzungsneutraler Flexibilität. Der Erschließungs- und Sanitärkern konzentriert sich in der Nordwestecke des Rechteckgrundrisses, alles andere ist mit Leichtbauwänden frei einteilbar, die fünf Stützen stören dabei wenig. Im obersten Geschoß wird die Mittelzone zusätzlich mit Oberlichtkuppeln aufgehellt. Pragmatik in Hinblick auf wechselnde Bedürfnisse der Nutzer und städtebauliche Vernunft, was das Äußere betrifft, finden an diesem Bau in positiver Weise zusammen.

The square two-story building, which is supported over the slightly recessed ground level by stilts, lies on the connecting road between Dornbirn and Lustenau, that also provides highway access. The rows of retail warehouses for cars, furniture, clothing etc, that went up quickly at the end of the 20th century give these high-incidence roads their specific aura of post-modern, auto-based urbanity. The smile shape of the building and its gray plaster finish have a pleasantly calm effect among the dozens of blatant signals and symbols that the area is flooded with. The glass-clad exterior addresses the contemporary need for a view of the sales space within. The closed gable ends of the upper levels, which appear to be a large vacant panel facing the street comments silently on its surroundings. Wide, elegantly proportioned windows are fitted along the lateral façades, which, however, do not upstage the importance of the walled surfaces. This gives the building its corporeal characteristics. What makes it special is the way it is both unspectacular yet memorable. This is achieved with the carefully balanced relationships between openings and closed wall surfaces and the effect of the mass on stilts as a whole that is not interrupted by any irregularities. On the other hand, the buildings' interior is defined by radical economy and a neutral flexibility of purpose. The installation and sanitary facilities are concentrated in the northwestern corner of the rectangular site plan and everything else can be sectioned freely with lightweight wall panels. The five girders are only minor hindrances. The middle segment of the uppermost level also receives additional light from skylight cupolas. A pragmatic attitude with regard to changing user needs and a reasonable approach to urban landscaping in terms of the exterior converge in a positive manner in this building.

2002
Dornbirn, Austria
Bauherrschaft | Client: Revital Bauträger GmbH, Dornbirn
Mitarbeit | Assistence: Francesco Capello, Gerhard Matt

Industrie- und Gewerbebauten / Industrial and Commercial Buildings

2. Obergeschoß
second floor

1. Obergeschoß
first floor

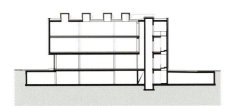

Längsschnitt
longitudinal section

Querschnitt
cross section

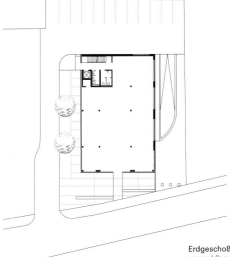

Erdgeschoß
ground floor

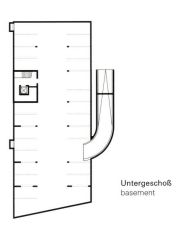

Untergeschoß
basement

Wohnanlagen
Housing Estates

Hermann Kaufmann

Wohnanlage Neudorfstraße, Wolfurt

Neudorfstraße Residential Projekt, Wolfurt

Die Wolfurter Neudorfstraße verläuft um Baublocktiefe nach Westen versetzt, parallel zur historischen Dorfstraße. Hinter der Straßenzeile aus jüngerer Bebauung liegt das Binnengrundstück, auf dem zwei parallele dreigeschoßige Gebäudetrakte einen breiten Zwischenraum definieren, durch den ein Fußgängerweg verläuft. Eine maßvolle Verdichtung der Siedlungsstruktur erfasst damit die ehemalige Gartenzone. Mit der Einbindung des Fußweges wird die neue Wohnanlage nach zwei Richtungen mit dem Dorf vernetzt. Die Südtypen sind über einen Laubengang im Norden erschlossen, das Treppenhaus wurde in den Baukörper integriert. Die Mitte nehmen Dreizimmerwohnungen ein, die – größeren – Vierzimmerwohnungen am westlichen und am östlichen Traktende nützen mit ihren Grundrissen die Möglichkeiten der Himmelsrichtungen. Sie sind äußerst kompakt organisiert, bieten aber unterschiedliche Möglichkeiten der Zimmerzuweisung. Damit wahrt der Wohnungsgrundriss Flexibilität gegenüber veränderten Bedingungen beim Älterwerden der Kinder. Vor der Südfassade stehen die Balkone, ihre Leichtbauweise in Stahl und Holzbohlen unterscheidet sie von den körperhaft mit einer Bretterschalung verkleideten, in Holzbauweise ebenfalls „leicht" errichteten Hauptvolumen. Im Norden weisen die schlank aufgestelzten Laubengänge eine kreuzungsfreundliche Breite auf; rasch zeigten sich da und dort individuelle Zeichen von Bewohntheit. Der Verzicht auf eine Tiefgarage erforderte zwar gedeckte Autoabstellplätze an der Oberfläche, sparte jedoch Kosten, was sich positiv auf die Mieten auswirkt. Im Gegensatz zu der vier Jahre früher entworfenen Wohnanlage Ölzbündt, wo ein patentiertes Bausystem entwickelt und erprobt wurde, ist das Konzept der Wolfurter Anlage von den meisten Zimmereien baubar, was ein offenes Angebotsverfahren ermöglichte. Für die Bauherrschaft war dies eine entscheidende Bedingung. Zwei weitere Anlagen werden zur Zeit gerade errichtet.

Neudorfstraße in Wolfurt runs parallel to the historically important Dorfstraße. The two streets are separated by the width of one building block. The construction site is located on an inside plot behind the row of recently constructed buildings on the street. Two parallel, three-story buildings define a broad interior space which is intersected by a pedestrian path. The measured density of the residential project's structure therefore also encompasses the former garden area. The integrated walkway links the project to the village in both directions. The southsides are connected by a path lined with deciduous trees to the north. The staircase was integrated into the structure. The middle segment of the structures are occupied by the three-room units, while the larger four-room apartments are located in the westerns and eastern wings, making use of the four points of the compass in their site plans. They are organized in a very compact fashion, but offer varying possibilities in terms of floor plan and room distribution. Hence the grounds plan makes concessions for changing circumstances as children get older, for example. The balconies are located in front of the southern façade. Their lightweight steel and timber plank construction sets them apart from the body of the main building, which was also completed using "light" construction methods. These included the use of timber cladding on the main building. To the north, the walkways framed by the slender supports of the deciduous trees offer a generous amount of space at the crossing that allowed for the quick emergence of signs of life. The decision to do without a subterranean garage made covered parking spaces on the surface necessary, but saved money, which had a positive effect on rent. As opposed to the Ölzbundt residential project designed and built a few years earlier using a patented construction technique that was tested and developed further during construction, the Wolfurt projects' elements can be supplied by most carpentry shops. This allows for open contracting competitions, which was one the contractor's prerequisites. Two additional projects are currently under construction.

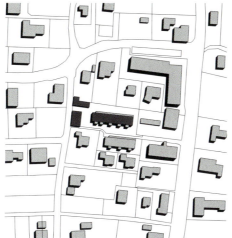

2001
Wolfurt, Austria
Bauherrschaft | Client: VOGEWOSI, Dornbirn
Mitarbeit | Assistence: Norbert Kaufmann, Wolfgang Bilgeri
Publikation | Publication: Holzbulletin, Mehrgeschoßiger Holzbau, 58/2001

Schnitt
section

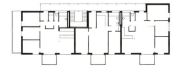

1. und 2. Obergeschoß
first and second floor

Erdgeschoß
ground floor

Untergeschoß
basement

0   10   20 m

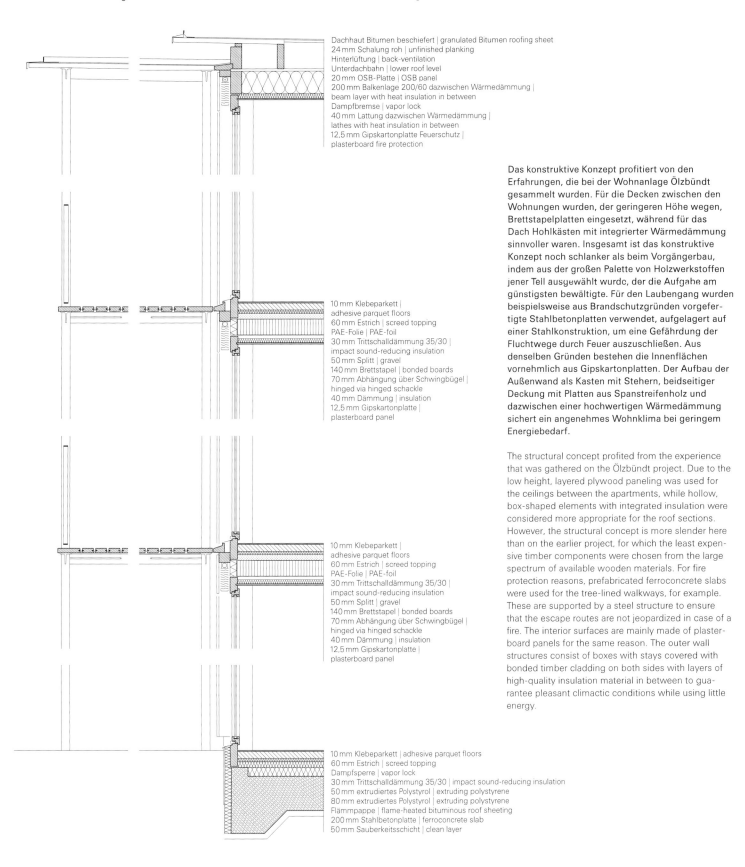

Das konstruktive Konzept profitiert von den Erfahrungen, die bei der Wohnanlage Ölzbündt gesammelt wurden. Für die Decken zwischen den Wohnungen wurden, der geringeren Höhe wegen, Brettstapelplatten eingesetzt, während für das Dach Hohlkästen mit integrierter Wärmedämmung sinnvoller waren. Insgesamt ist das konstruktive Konzept noch schlanker als beim Vorgängerbau, indem aus der großen Palette von Holzwerkstoffen jener Teil ausgewählt wurde, der die Aufgabe am günstigsten bewältigte. Für den Laubengang wurden beispielsweise aus Brandschutzgründen vorgefertigte Stahlbetonplatten verwendet, aufgelagert auf einer Stahlkonstruktion, um eine Gefährdung der Fluchtwege durch Feuer auszuschließen. Aus denselben Gründen bestehen die Innenflächen vornehmlich aus Gipskartonplatten. Der Aufbau der Außenwand als Kasten mit Stehern, beidseitiger Deckung mit Platten aus Spanstreifenholz und dazwischen einer hochwertigen Wärmedämmung sichert ein angenehmes Wohnklima bei geringem Energiebedarf.

The structural concept profited from the experience that was gathered on the Ölzbündt project. Due to the low height, layered plywood paneling was used for the ceilings between the apartments, while hollow, box-shaped elements with integrated insulation were considered more appropriate for the roof sections. However, the structural concept is more slender here than on the earlier project, for which the least expensive timber components were chosen from the large spectrum of available wooden materials. For fire protection reasons, prefabricated ferroconcrete slabs were used for the tree-lined walkways, for example. These are supported by a steel structure to ensure that the escape routes are not jeopardized in case of a fire. The interior surfaces are mainly made of plasterboard panels for the same reason. The outer wall structures consist of boxes with stays covered with bonded timber cladding on both sides with layers of high-quality insulation material in between to guarantee pleasant climactic conditions while using little energy.

Hermann Kaufmann

Wohnanlage Ölzbündt, Dornbirn
Ölzbündt Residential Project, Dornbirn

Die Bündt, von althochdeutsch biunt(a), bezeichnet in Süddeutschland, der Schweiz und eben in Vorarlberg den – gegen Wildverbiss – eingezäunten Gemüsegarten nahe dem Haus. So steht denn der lange Baukörper auf einem Handtuchgrundstück im Binnenbereich eines Gevierts, dessen Rand von Einfamilienhäusern besetzt ist, an der nordöstlichen Peripherie von Dornbirn. Der längsquadrische Dreigeschoßer ist mit einer Lärchenstülpschalung verkleidet, womit das Volumen betont wird. Die Balkone vor der Westseite und die Laubengänge an der Ostseite sind aus schlanken Stahlprofilen und Holzplatten errichtet und davorgestellt. Hauptbaukörper und angefügte Außenbereiche sind damit strukturell klar unterschieden. Als drittes Element kommt das Treppenhaus dazu, dessen Eigenständigkeit eine Hülle aus Profilglas unterstreicht. Den Südkopf besetzt ein in die Großform integriertes Einfamilienhaus. Außen ist eine Raumschicht mehrgeschoßiger Balkone davorgelegt. Im Inneren ist es schall- und brandschutztechnisch durch eine Betonmauer vom Geschoßwohnungsteil geschieden. Die zwölf Wohnungen sind kompakt organisiert. Sie weisen je zur Hälfte zwei beziehungsweise drei Zimmer auf, und jede verfügt über einen die ganze Trakttiefe nützenden großen Raum für Wohnen-Kochen-Essen. Die schmalhohen Fenster mit tiefen Leibungen und die fast 0,5 Meter starken Außenwände verleihen dem Gebäude trotz der kostengünstigen Konstruktionsweise einen soliden Charakter. Holz ist hier nicht für provisorische Zwecke, sondern dauerhaft eingesetzt. Zusätzlich zur Wahl der witterungsbeständigen Lärche für die äußerste Schicht dient ein ausladendes Vordach als Wetterschirm über der Fassade, um die Haltbarkeit auch ohne Holzschutzmittel zu verlängern. Die Zufahrt zur unterirdischen Einstellhalle und der Zugang zur Treppe erfolgen von Norden. Vom obersten Laubengang führt jedoch ein Weg über eine Treppe und einen Steg nach Süden. Über ihn ist das Haus auch nach dieser Seite mit dem Quartier vernetzt.

Ölzbündt, from the old German word biunt(a), is a word used in Southern Germany, Switzerland and Vorarlberg for a vegetable garden that is fenced in close to a house to protect it from wild animals roaming free. Thus the long structure lies on a narrow plot on the interior of a zone whose edge is lined with single-family houses on the northeastern outskirts of Dornbirn. The square, elongated three-story building is clad with larch wood weather boarding that emphasizes the structure's volume. The balconies on the western side and the tree-lined walkways are made of slender steel struts with timber planking in front, hence the main structure and adjacent outer spaces can be clearly differentiated. The stairway is the third structural element. Its individuality is underlined by a bent glass shell. A single family residential unit that is integrated in the large overall shape occupies the southern segment. A layer of exterior space was added to the building in form of multi-level balconies. On the inside, the residential floor section is protected against fire and acoustically insulated by a cement wall. The twelve apartments are compactly organized. Each of the units has either two or three rooms and all apartments feature a large room that makes use of the wings, full depth for cooking, dining and living. The narrow tall windows with their deep sills and the almost 0.5 meter thick outer walls give the building a massive feeling despite the cost-efficient construction method that was used. Timber is not intended for provisional purposes here, it is meant for sustained use. In addition to the larch wood timber used on the weather boarding, the building also features a projecting canopy roof that acts as protection against the weather for the façade, in order to prolong its lifecycle without using protective wood additives. Access to the subterranean parking garage and the stairs is possible from the north. However, a path leads from the uppermost tree-lined walkway over a staircase and bridge to the south as well. The building is also linked with its surroundings on this side.

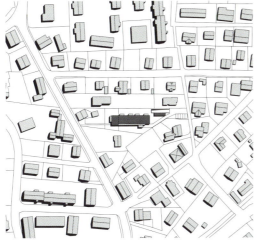

1997
Dornbirn, Austria
Bauherrschaft | Client: Anton Kaufmann, Reuthe; Gerold Ölz, Dornbirn
Energiekonzept | Energetic concept: Bernd Kraus
Mitarbeit | Assistence: Norbert Kaufmann, Wolfgang Elmenreich
Publikation | Publication: baumeister 10/1997; Architektur Aktuell, 209, 11/1997; Mehrgeschoßiger Holzhausbau, Ott Verlag, Thun, 1997; Hochparterre Nr. 3, März 1998; architektur, holzbau, 4/1998; DBZ dt. Bauzeitschrift, April 1999; Wohnmodell Bayern, kostengünstiger Wohnbau, Callwey 1999; Bois et environnement, Nr. 32, Oktober 2000; Architektur und Wohnen, 03/2001; Holzbulletin Mehrgeschoßiger Holzbau, 59/2001

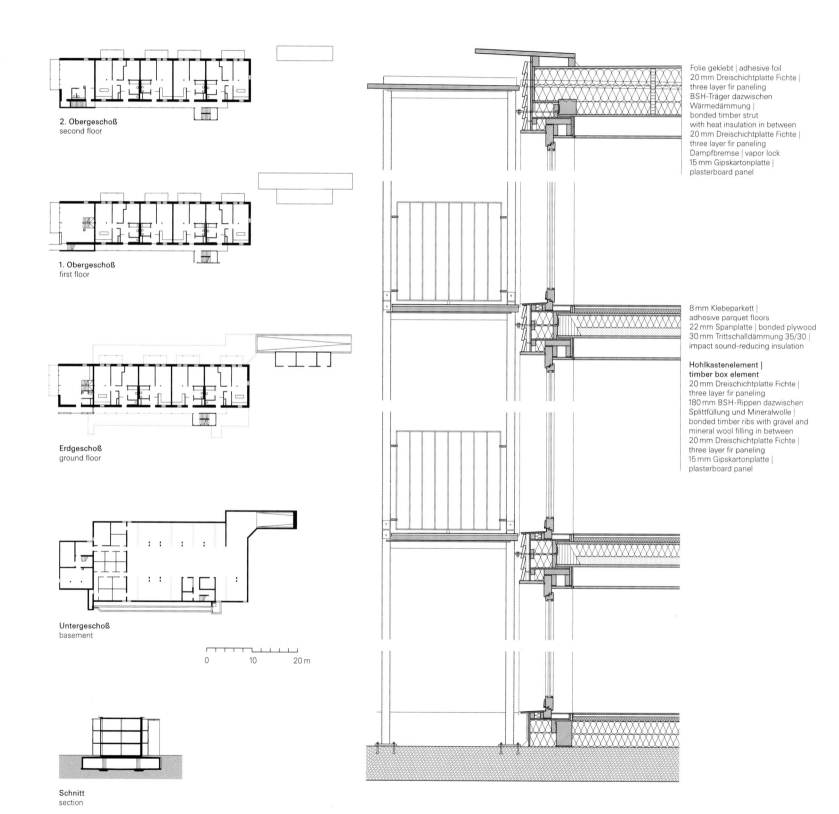

Folie geklebt | adhesive foil
20 mm Dreischichtplatte Fichte |
three layer fir paneling
BSH-Träger dazwischen Wärmedämmung |
bonded timber strut with heat insulation in between
20 mm Dreischichtplatte Fichte |
three layer fir paneling
Dampfbremse | vapor lock
15 mm Gipskartonplatte | plasterboard panel

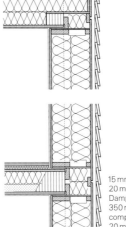

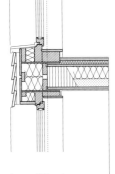

8 mm Klebeparkett | adhesive parquet floors
22 mm Spanplatte | bonded plywood
30 mm Trittschalldämmung 35/30 |
impact sound-reducing insulation

Hohlkastenelement | timber box element
20 mm Dreischichtplatte Fichte |
three layer fir paneling
180 mm BSH-Rippen dazwischen
Splittfüllung und Mineralwolle |
bonded timber ribs with gravel and
mineral wool filling in between
20 mm Dreischichtplatte Fichte |
three layer fir paneling
15 mm Gipskartonplatte | plasterboard panel

15 mm Gipskartonplatte | plasterboard panel
20 mm Spanplatte | bonded plywood
Dampfbremse | vapor lock
350 mm Verbundsteher dazwischen Wärmedämmung |
composite strut with heat insulation in between
20 mm Spanplatte | bonded plywood
40 mm Konterlattung | counter lathes
Stülpschalung Lärche | weather boarding larch

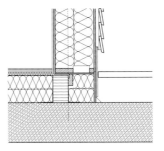

 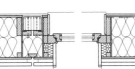 

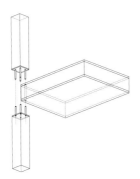

Der dreigeschoßige, integrale Holzbau besteht vornehmlich aus Holzwerkstoffen, die in Werkstattfertigung zu Elementen gefügt als Bausystem mit einem Rastermaß von 2,40 Metern mit großem Zeitgewinn auf der Baustelle zusammengesetzt wurden. Brettschichtholz, Dreischichtplatten, Spanplatten, Verbundstegträger, auch Massivholzbretter fanden nach Maßgabe ihrer statisch-konstruktiven Eigenschaften, ihrer Witterungsbeständigkeit, selbst gestalterischer Kriterien an der ihnen angemessenen Stelle Verwendung, wobei ökonomische Überlegungen wesentlich mitspielten. Zur Schalldämmung wurde Split in die Hohlkästen der Deckenelemente eingefüllt, und aus Brand-

schutzgründen kam beim Innenausbau Gipska zur Anwendung. Dank der guten Wärmedämm der Außenwände konnte auf Heizkörper verzic werden. Mit individuell steuerbarer, kontrollier Lüftung, Wärmetauscher und Restenergienutz werden im Schnitt nicht mehr als 25 kWh pro Quadratmeter und Jahr verbraucht. Sonnenko toren auf dem Dach erzeugen das Warmwasse

Housing Estates

The three-story, integral timber structure is primarily made of wood components that were finished as construction system elements by a workshop for a grid measuring 2.40 meters. This allowed them to be assembled quickly on-site. Bonded timber panels, thee-layer panels, plywood and solid timber planking were employed according to their structural characteristics, weather resilience and even design criteria. Economic considerations also played a major role in these decisions. The hollow, box-shaped roof elements were filled with gravel for sound damping and plasterboard panels were used on the interior. Heating elements were not necessary due to the good heat insulating properties of the outer walls. No more than 26 kWh/Btu per square meter and year are necessary since the building features individually adjustable ventilation, heat exchangers and uses residual energy efficiently. Sun panels on the roof furnish warm water.

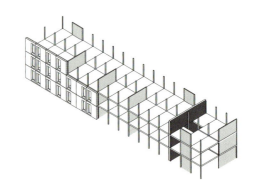

Das Energiekonzept nützt die bestens gedämmte, dichte sowie wärmebrückenfreie Gebäudehülle und ermöglicht ein Heizen über Zuluft innerhalb des Mindestluftwechsels. Individuell steuerbare Kompaktgeräte in jeder Wohnung sorgen für Lüftung und Heizung. Frische Außenluft wird im Erdwärmetauscher auf mindestens 0°C vortemperiert. Nutzung der Abluftwärme bis zu 60% mittels Plattenwärmetauscher. Eine Kleinstwärmepumpe erhöht die Zulufttemperatur auf maximal 40°C. Stoßlüftung durch Fenster ist weiterhin möglich.

The energy concept makes use of the very well insulated, sealed and thermal bridge free building shell, making it possible to heat incoming air even if it is a minimal amount of air that is circulated. Compact, individually adjustable devices control the ventilation and heating in every apartment. Fresh air is heated to minimum of 0° centigrade by the geothermic heat exchanger in each building. Up to 60 per cent of the residual heat can be recycled via a plate heat exchanger. A small heating pump increase the incoming air temperature to a maximum of 40° centigrade. However, it is still possible to vent additional air via the windows.

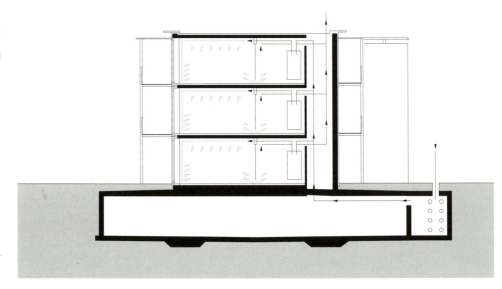

Christian Lenz

Wohnanlage Dammstraße, Schwarzach
Dammstraße Residential Project, Schwarzach

Mit ihrem Damm teilt die Bahnlinie die landwirtschaftlich genutzten Riedflächen der Rheintalebene. In einem großen Bogen nähert sie sich bis auf einen halben Kilometer dem Dorf. „Vor" oder „hinter dem Damm" benennt da verschiedene Welten. Aber dort, wo sich Bahn, Schwarzach und ein Sträßchen, das irgendwo im Ried als Pfad endet, kreuzen, ist dennoch ein unverwechselbarer Ort konkreter Poesie entstanden. Geschoßwohnungsbau muss mit günstigen Mieten aufwarten in einem Land, in dem das eigene Haus der Normalfall ist. Die spartanischen Konsequenzen für den Entwurf lauteten daher: Verzicht auf ein Untergeschoß, Laubengangerschließung, offene Treppen, kompakte Grundrisse. Zwei parallele Baukörper, die Längsfassaden nach Südwesten gerichtet und die Rücken leicht schräg zur Hauptlärmquelle gedreht, bilden die dreigeschoßige Wohnanlage. Die Abstellräume sind zu autonomen dreigeschoßigen Volumen zusammengefasst, zugänglich über Stege am Ende der Laubengänge. Gleichsam trotzig bestimmen sie als lattenverkleidete Türme die Ansicht von der Bahn. In den Kopfteilen der beiden Baukörper sind jeweils die größeren Wohnungen angeordnet, damit die günstige Orientierung für die Fenster der Kinderzimmer genutzt werden kann. Die – lärmigere – Laubengangseite ist karg und abschirmend, während auf der Hauptwohnseite breite Balkone mit farbigen Brüstungen aus Faserzementplatten ein fröhliches Bild vermitteln. Helle Mauerscheiben umfassen von beiden Seiten den „weichen" Abschnitt der Fensterwände mit den davor befindlichen Balkonen. Die Zwei-, Drei- und wenigen Vierzimmer-Wohnungen weisen eine Standardausstattung auf mit Vorraum, Küche, Bad, Wohnraum und Zimmer/n. Im Erdgeschoß verfügen sie über einen eigenen Gartenplatz, in den Obergeschoßen erlaubt der zwei Meter tiefe Balkon von zehn Quadratmetern Fläche ein ansprechendes Außenwohnen. Selbst für den extrem kostengünstigen Wohnbau gelingt es, mit der klaren äußeren Form, dem Farbenspiel und den unverwechselbaren Holztürmen Identität zu schaffen, die ein Wohnen auch an diesem Ort zu mehr als einem gerade erträglichen Übergangszustand machen.

The railway dam divides meadowy areas of the Rhine Valley that are used for agricultural purposes. It traces a broad curve before coming stopping half a kilometer away from the village. "Vor" or "Hinter dem Damm" (Before or After the Dam) defines the difference between two worlds. However a place of unmistakable poetry was created at the intersection between the railway, Schwarzach and a little road that ends as a dirt path. Multi-story apartment buildings have offer appealing tenancy fees in an are in which single-family houses are the norm. This lead to the Spartan decision to do without a cellar level and the use of walkways lined with deciduous trees, open staircases and compact site plans. Two parallel buildings were built with their longitudinal façades facing southwest with their backs turned slightly away from the main source of noise. These structures constitute the three-level residential project. The storage rooms are accumulated in an autonomous three-story building that can be reached via bridges at the end of the tree-lined walkways. At the same time, their lattice-clad appearance defiantly defines the view of the railway. The larger apartments are located in the front sections of both buildings, making use of the advantageous lie to locate the children's room's windows. The louder side facing the tree-lined walkways is bleak and forbidding, while the main living section is enlivened with the balconies that feature colorful balustrades made of cement reinforced fiberboard. Lightly shaded wall panels cover both sides of the "soft" window segment behind the balconies. The two, three and few four-room units are equipped with standard features such as the foyer, kitchen, bathroom, living area and room(s). The lower levels feature individual garden spaces, while the upper levels are equipped with ten sqm balconies that are two meters deep, creating an appealing outer space. Even this extremely cost-efficient residential building succeeds in defining its own identity with its clear exterior form, the interplay of color and the unmistakable timber towers that makes this more than a merely tolerable transitional living space.

1996
Schwarzach, Austria
Bauherrschaft | Client: Revital Bauträger GmbH, Dornbirn
Mitarbeit | Assistence: Jürgen Erath
Publikation | Publication: Baukunst in Vorarlberg seit 1980, Kunsthaus Bregenz, VAI, 1998

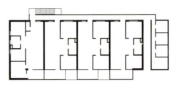

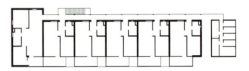

2. Obergeschoß
second floor

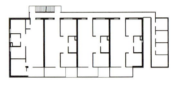

Querschnitt 2
cross section 2

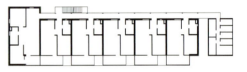

1. Obergeschoß
first floor

Querschnitt 1
cross section 1

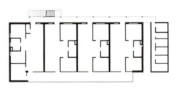

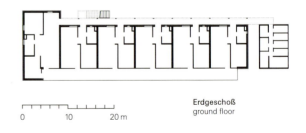

Erdgeschoß
ground floor

0   10   20 m

Christian Lenz

Wohnanlage Weidachstraße, Schwarzach

Weidachstraße Housing Project, Schwarzach

Nördlich des Dorfkerns, in der Zone der Obstgärten, wird mit dem kräftigen viergeschoßigen Baukörper eine maßvolle Verdichtung der lockeren Bebauungsstruktur angestrebt. Der weiße, massiv gebaute Quader wird von den Öffnungen der französischen Fenster mit einem rhythmischen Raster überzogen. Diesem regelmäßigen Muster sind dunkelrot akzentuierte, loggienartige Volumen appliziert, die teils in den Hauptbaukörper eingeschnitten sind, teils auskragen. Mit diesem größermaschigen Muster, das nur jedes zweite Geschoß erfasst, wird eine Differenzierung der Grundfolie des Fensterrasters erreicht. Besonders die Ecken werden von der verdoppelnden Betonung, die zuoberst mit einem räumlichen Herausschneiden einhergeht, im Ausdruck stark verändert. Ein Blick auf die innere Gliederung zeigt, dass die Anordnung der Loggien keineswegs bloß formalistische Spielerei ist. Die durchdachte Mischung aus Geschoßwohnungen und Maisonnetten nützt die Vorteile jeder Lage und erlaubt das Spiel mit dem Maßstabssprung. Im Erdgeschoß haben die drei großen Wohnungen für Familien mit Kindern je Zugang zu einem individuellen Gartenteil. Das erste Obergeschoß enthält mehrheitlich kleine Wohnungen, die jeweils über eine Loggia verfügen. Die oberen beiden Geschoße werden von einem Kranz aus sechs Maisonnetten gebildet, in denen die Schlafräume unten und die Wohnräume oben angeordnet sind. Die Loggien werden zu Dachterrassen, die in den Baukörper eingesenkt und deren abstrakte Volumen durch Pergolen definiert sind. Den großen Kern des Gebäudes bildet ein räumlich großzügiges Treppenhaus mit galerieartigen Gängen, von denen aus die Wohnungen zugänglich sind. Nach Maßgabe der Notwendigkeiten werden in den oberen beiden Geschoßen größere Deckenteile weggelassen, sodass Tageslicht durch das Glasdach flutet und bis ins Erdgeschoß hinunter zu dringen vermag. Auch wenn die Treppe neben dem Aufzug funktional zweitrangig sein mag, architektonisch wird der Raum kraftvoll belebt, der Weg zur Wohnung gewinnt an Attraktivität und wertet diese auf.

The objective of the powerful, four-story building in the orchard area north of the village center, is to add an adequate sense of density to the loosely developed surroundings. The white, solidly built square is given a rhythmic grid by the French windows. Volume was added to this uniform pattern by applying partly projecting loggia-like sections that were cut into the main building. This loosely-knit structuring affects every second floor, allowing for a differentiation from the contrasting grid of windows. The corners are particularly affected by this double emphasis, which is accompanied by the spatial excision at the top. A glance at the interior organization shows that the alignment of the loggias wasn't merely a play on forms. The well-considered blend between an apartment and duplexes takes advantage of every location and allows for the use of varying scales. On the ground floor, the three large apartments for families with children feature access to their own individual garden spaces. The first upper level mainly contains small apartments, which each have their own loggia. Both upper levels are constituted by a wreath of duplexes which have their bedrooms below and the living spaces on the uppermost level. Hence the loggias become rooftop terraces imbedded in the structure whose abstract volume is defined by pergolas. A generously-dimensioned stairwell with gallery-like halls leading to the apartments constitutes the core of the building. After gauging the necessity, it was decided that it was preferable to allow daylight to stream into the building, right down to the ground floor via the glass ceiling rather than use large roof panels. Although the stairs are only of secondary functional importance next to the elevator they add liveliness to the space and heighten the appeal of reaching the individual apartments.

2002
Schwarzach, Austria
Bauherrschaft | Client: Revital Bauträger GmbH, Dornbirn
Mitarbeit | Assistence: Susanne Dünser, Rudolf Sommer, Helmut Brunner

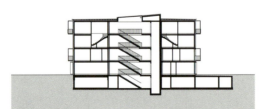
Längsschnitt
longitudinal section

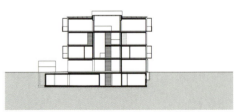
Querschnitt
cross section

0   10   20 m

Dachgeschoß
top floor

2. Obergeschoß
second floor

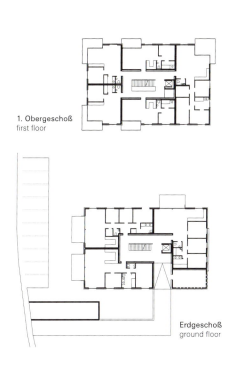

1. Obergeschoß
first floor

Erdgeschoß
ground floor

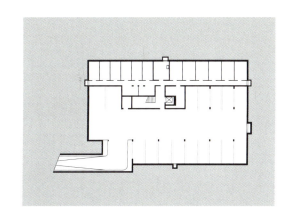

Untergeschoß
basement

Kies | grave
Folie | foil
20 mm Schalung | paneling
200 mm Wärmedämmung | heat insulation
Dampfsperre | vapor lock
260 mm Stahlbeton | ferroconcrete
10 mm Putz | plaster

14 mm Parkett | parquet
60 mm Estrich | screed topping
Folie | foil
50 mm Trittschalldämmung 55/50 | impact sound-reducing insulation
30 mm Kiesschüttung | gravel filling
260 mm Stahlbeton | ferroconcrete
10 mm Putz | plaster

Lattenrost | lattice grid
Gummischrot | rubber gravel
Folie | foil
OSB-Platte im Gefälle | sloping OSB panel
Holzkonstruktion dazwischen
Wärmedämmung | timber construction with heat insulation in between
Dampfsperre | vapor lock
260 mm Stahlbeton | ferroconcrete
10 mm Putz | plaster

beschichtetes Blech | coaded sheet metal
100 mm Dübelholz | dowel timber

14 mm Parkett | parquet
60 mm Estrich | screed topping
Folie | foil
50 mm Trittschalldämmung 55/50 | impact sound-reducing insulation
30 mm Kiesschüttung | gravel filling
260 mm Stahlbeton | ferroconcrete
100 mm Wärmedämmung | heat insulation
10 mm Putz | plaster

14 mm Parkett | parquet
60 mm Estrich | screed topping
Folie | foil
50 mm Trittschalldämmung 55/50 | impact sound-reducing insulation
30 mm Kiesschüttung | gravel filling
260 mm Stahlbeton | ferroconcrete
10 mm Putz | plaster

30 mm Lattenrost
Lattung | lathes
50 mm Luftraum | airspace
10 mm Gummimatte | rubber mat
Dachhaut (Folie) | roofing sheet (foil)
80 mm Lattung dazwischen Wärmedämmung | lathes with heat insulation in between
130 mm Wärmedämmung | heat insulation
Dampfsperre | vapor lock
260 mm Stahlbeton | ferroconcrete
10 mm Putz | plaster

14 mm Parkett | parquet
60 mm Estrich | screed topping
Dampfbremse | vapor lock
130 mm Dämmschüttung | insulation filling
450 mm Stahlbeton | ferroconcrete
55 mm Dämmung | insulation

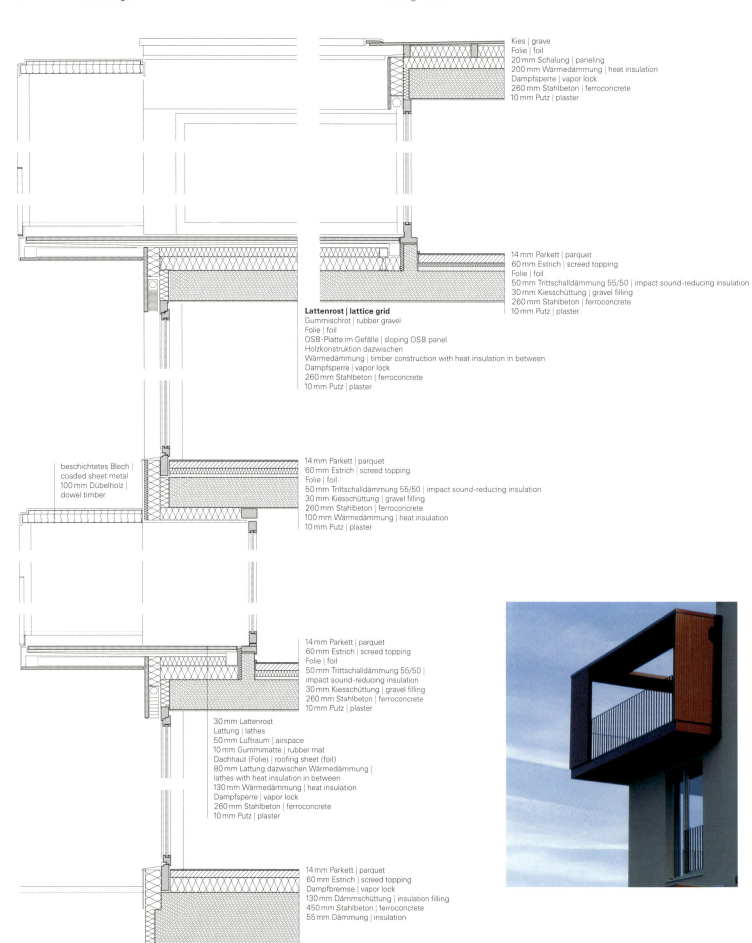

Einfamilienhäuser
Single-Family Houses

Hermann Kaufmann

Haus Beck-Faigle, Hard
House Beck-Faigle, Hard

Das Haufendorf Hard liegt westlich der Mündung der Bregenzer Ach am Deltarand zum Bodensee. In der lockeren und wenig strukturierten Bebauung befindet sich das Grundstück nahe der Dorfmitte. Ein altes Häuschen und ein Apfelbaum standen darauf. Ihre Entfernung wurde nicht nur verworfen, vielmehr diente der Bestand dem Entwurf als Ansatz. Ein neues, kräftiges Winkelelement aus einer hochgedämmten Holzkonstruktion wurde knapp an die nördliche und die östliche Grundgrenze gerückt. In die offene Ecke schmiegt sich ein einfacher Quader, sodass deren Flügel markant über das Volumen hinausstehen. Die südliche Gartenhälfte bleibt frei, während der Apfelbaum im neuen Gartenhof vor dem Wohnraum den Außensitzplatz beschattet. Das erneuerte Häuschen dient als Wirtschaftsraum und Werkstatt sowie zum Abstellen des Autos. Das erlaubte im ohnehin hoch liegenden Grundwasser kostensenkend auf einen Keller zu verzichten. Ein Dach verbindet das Häuschen mit dem Haus. Dessen Zugang führt nun durch den von Alt und Neu gebildeten Eingangshof im Westen, wo ein breites Vordach den Raum abschließt und Besucher wie Heimkehrende freundlich Willkommen heißt. Der kompakte Grundriss kombiniert im Erdgeschoß Kochen, Essen, Wohnen und Nebenräume sowie ein Studio, während oben drei Schlafzimmer, das Bad und eine großzügige Diele, die als Bibliothek dient, vom geraden Lauf der Treppe erschlossen werden. Gebaut wurde vor allem mit Holzwerkstoffen, nur Boden und Rückwandverkleidung sind aus massiven Lärchenbrettern gefügt. In die Konstruktion des bergenden Winkels, dessen architektonische Rolle der eines ausladenden Daches verwandt ist, sind nur wenige und kleine Fenster geschnitten. Garten- und Eingangsseite wurden hingegen vollflächig verglast. Hinter Glasbrüstungen und geschlossenen Fassadenteilen befindet sich eine Kartonwabendämmung mit Pufferwirkung. Dach und Betonfundament sind ebenfalls stark gedämmt, sodass der Heizenergieverbrauch 24 kWh pro Quadratmeter und Jahr unterschreitet. Ein Pelletofen wärmt den Wohnbereich, Hypokausten im Obergeschoß sowie die Zuluft der kontrollierten Lüftung.

Hard, the haphazardly developed village in the area, lies to the west of the mouth of the Bregenzer Ach River on the edge of the Lake Constance Delta. The plot is located close to the middle of the sparsely and loosely developed village. A little old house and apple tree were formerly located here. Rather than being removed, their existence served to create the structural approach. A new, strong angular highly insulated timber element was placed close to the northern and eastern site borders. A simple square occupies the open corner, with wings that project strikingly beyond the volume of the space. The southern garden half remained free, while the apple tree provides shadow in the courtyard for the outside living space in front of the residential unit. The renovated little house now serves as a commercial area, workshop and parking space. This made it possible to do without a cellar, which would have been expensive to build due to the high ground water level in the area. A roof connects the little house with the building. This entryway leads the visitor through the forecourt composed of old and new elements to the west, where a broad canopy encloses the space, welcoming visitors as if they were returning home. The compact floor plan combines eating, cooking, living and service areas as well as a studio on the ground floor. The upper level includes three bedrooms, the bathroom and a generous hall that serves as a library. Access to all of these rooms is possible via the straight staircase. Construction was mainly completed with timber components. Massive larch wood timber components were only used on the floors and back wall paneling. Only a limited number of small windows were built into the angular structure of the building, which serves as a projecting roof. On the other hand, the garden and entrance side features complete glass cladding. Buffering cardboard honeycomb insulation lies behind the glass ledges and enclosed façade surfaces. The roof and cement foundation also feature major insulation, which keeps heating energy consumption at under 24 KWH/Btu per square meter and year. A pellet-fed furnace heats the residential area and hypocaust channels on the upper level control both the heating and air circulation.

1998
Hard, Austria
Bauherrschaft | Client: Ursula Beck-Faigle und Wolfgang Beck, Hard
Mitarbeit | Assistence: Richard Forer, Christoph Kalb

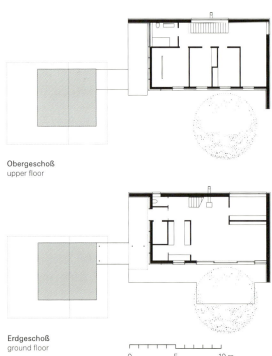

Obergeschoß
upper floor

Erdgeschoß
ground floor

0 5 10 m

Querschnitt
cross section

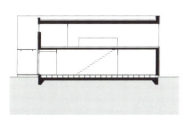

Längsschnitt
longitudinal section

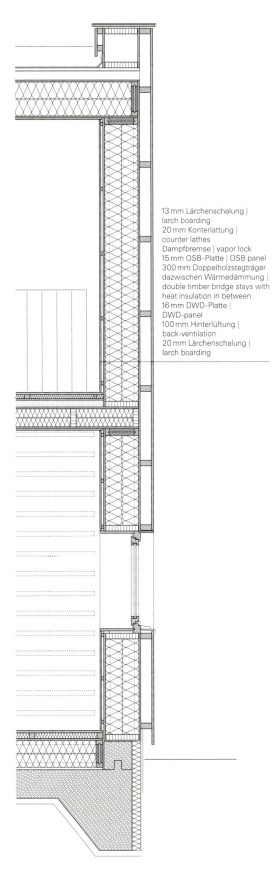

13 mm Lärchenschalung | larch boarding
20 mm Konterlattung | counter lathes
Dampfbremse | vapor lock
15 mm OSB-Platte | OSB panel
300 mm Doppelholzstegträger dazwischen Wärmedämmung | double timber bridge stays with heat insulation in between
16 mm DWD-Platte | DWD-panel
100 mm Hinterlüftung | back-ventilation
20 mm Lärchenschalung | larch boarding

Einfamilienhäuser — Single-Family Houses

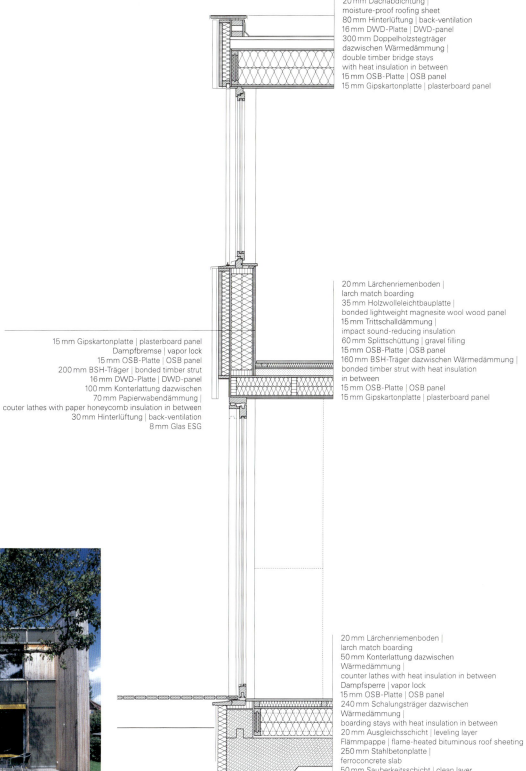

20 mm Dachabdichtung |
moisture-proof roofing sheet
80 mm Hinterlüftung | back-ventilation
16 mm DWD-Platte | DWD-panel
300 mm Doppelholzstegträger
dazwischen Wärmedämmung |
double timber bridge stays
with heat insulation in between
15 mm OSB-Platte | OSB panel
15 mm Gipskartonplatte | plasterboard panel

15 mm Gipskartonplatte | plasterboard panel
Dampfbremse | vapor lock
15 mm OSB-Platte | OSB panel
200 mm BSH-Träger | bonded timber strut
16 mm DWD-Platte | DWD-panel
100 mm Konterlattung dazwischen
70 mm Papierwabendämmung |
couter lathes with paper honeycomb insulation in between
30 mm Hinterlüftung | back-ventilation
8 mm Glas ESG

20 mm Lärchenriemenboden |
larch match boarding
35 mm Holzwolleleichtbauplatte |
bonded lightweight magnesite wool wood panel
15 mm Trittschalldämmung |
impact sound-reducing insulation
60 mm Splittschüttung | gravel filling
15 mm OSB-Platte | OSB panel
160 mm BSH-Träger dazwischen Wärmedämmung |
bonded timber strut with heat insulation
in between
15 mm OSB-Platte | OSB panel
15 mm Gipskartonplatte | plasterboard panel

20 mm Lärchenriemenboden |
larch match boarding
50 mm Konterlattung dazwischen
Wärmedämmung |
counter lathes with heat insulation in between
Dampfsperre | vapor lock
15 mm OSB-Platte | OSB panel
240 mm Schalungsträger dazwischen
Wärmedämmung |
boarding stays with heat insulation in between
20 mm Ausgleichsschicht | leveling layer
Flämmpappe | flame-heated bituminous roof sheeting
250 mm Stahlbetonplatte |
ferroconcrete slab
50 mm Sauberkeitsschicht | clean layer

Hermann Kaufmann

Haus Anton Kaufmann, Reuthe

House Anton Kaufmann, Reuthe

Der zurückhaltende Neubau zählt zur Häusergruppe zwischen Vorder Reuthe und Hinter Reuthe und befindet sich auf der Hangschulter über der Klus der Bregenzer Ach, an der alten Verbindungsstraße nach Mellau. Die attraktive Südlage wird im Norden von einem Waldsaum geschützt. Auf einem quer stehenden, massiv aus Stahlbeton errichteten Eingangsgeschoß mit Büro, Doppelgarage und Treppenhalle lagert der längsquadrische Baukörper des Obergeschoßes auf und kragt sogar kühn, den Eingang beschirmend, vor. In innovativer Holzbauweise errichtet, beherbergt er die Wohn- und die Schlafräume. Aus dem großzügigen Entree gelangt man über die elegant geschwungene Treppe in eine weiträumige Diele. Sie teilt den Grundriss: Die Kinderzimmer liegen im östlich auskragenden Gebäudeteil. Nach Westen schließt eine große Wohnzone an, vom körperhaften Ofen geteilt in Essplatz und Sitzgruppe, versorgt von einer geräumigen Küche. Dahinter folgt der Elternschlafbereich im westlichen Gebäudeteil. Das gesamte Wohngeschoß ist südseitig mit wandhohen Schiebefenstern versehen. Ein rahmenartig vorstehender, flacher Balkon zieht sich über die Fassade, fasst sie zusammen und trägt die außen angesetzten, verschiebbaren Läden, deren Leistenroste die großen Glasflächen beschatten und die Räume vor Blicken schützen. Das begrünte Dach des Sockelgeschoßes weist vor der Wohndiele eine große Holzplattform auf, die, bestens besonnt, dem Außenwohnen dient. Das Haus ist aus wärmegedämmten Hohlkästen konstruiert, wobei für die Rippen zwischen den Holzwerkstoffplatten Stegträger aus hauseigener Produktion der Kaufmann-Werke eingesetzt wurden, wie sie im Schalungsbau üblich sind. Von diesem rigorosen und kostensparenden Pragmatismus ist allerdings an der eleganten äußeren Erscheinung nichts mehr zu bemerken.

The restrained new building belongs to the group of buildings that lies between Vorder Reuthe and Hinter Reuthe and is located on the shoulder overlooking the Bregenzer Ach River, on the old connecting road to Mellau. the forest on the northern edge protects the attractive southern location of the site. The square, elongated upper level structure rests on the massive, horizontally aligned ferroconcrete ground level structure that includes office, spaces, a double garage and stairwell. The upper level projects forward, boldly covering the entrance. It was built using innovative timber construction techniques and contains the living and bedrooms. From the generously proportioned entrance, the visitor gains access to an ample hall via an elegantly curved stairway. This serves to divide the floor plan: the children's rooms are located in the building section that projects towards the east. A large living area that is separated into a living and dining room by a furnace follows to the west. This space also features a roomy kitchen. Behind it lie the adult's bedrooms it in the western building segment. The entire residential level features floor-to-ceiling sliding windows. A frame-like, projecting flat balcony covers the façade and supports the sliding panels mounted on the outside. The ledges and strip gratings of these panels create shadows on the glass surfaces and protect the rooms from inquisitive glances. The greenery-covered roof of the base course continues as a large timber platform in front of the pantry. It receives ample sunlight and is therefore useful as outside living space. The building was constructed with hollow-box-shaped, insulated elements and the bridging elements between the timber plywood bridging components were conceived and produced at the Kaufmann-Werke according to conventional formwork principles. However, none of this rigorous, cost-cutting pragmatism is visible or noticeable on the structure's elegant exterior.

1998
Reuthe, Austria
Bauherrschaft | Client: Anton Kaufmann, Reuthe
Mitarbeit | Assistence: Stefan Hiebeler

Obergeschoß
upper floor

Untergeschoß
basement

0   5   10 m

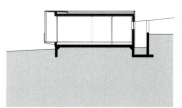

Querschnitt 1
cross section 1

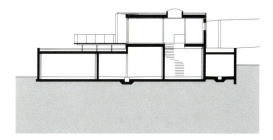

Querschnitt 2
cross section 2

Hermann Kaufmann

Haus Fuchs, Langen bei Bregenz

House Fuchs, Langen near Bregenz

Das talseitig zweigeschoßige Wohnhaus steht in 720 Meter Seehöhe auf einem alten Hausplatz über dem Dorf. Von der nach Südosten gerichteten, oben bewaldeten Bergflanke ist die Aussicht auf die felsigen, winters verschneiten Ketten des Bregenzerwaldes kaum zu überbieten. Das ausladende, flache Dach beschirmt und beschattet zwei Baukörper, eine offene Zwischenzone und einen umlaufenden Balkon. Der kleinere, dessen geschlossene Stirnseite Ankommende als Erstes sehen, enthält oben die Doppelgarage und darunter eine Sauna. Der breite Zwischenbereich mit Treppenabgang zur Gartenterrasse bildet einen gedeckten Eingangsvorraum zum größeren Baukörper, der oben Kochen-Essen-Wohnen sowie ein Studio enthält und unten die Schlafräume nebst ausreichend bemessenen Serviceräumen. Der Grundriss ist in hangparallele Schichten strukturiert: zuvorderst der flache Balkon, dann die dreiseitig verglasten Wohnräume, hernach die Neben- und Sanitärräume; zuhinterst, bereits unter der Erde des ansteigenden Berghanges, bilden Technik- und Kellerräume ein längsprismatisches Verbindungselement für beide Teile. Nach Südwesten weist die Balkonplattform gut drei Meter Tiefe auf und dient als Außensitzplatz. Konstruktiv wirken im rückwärtigen Bereich kräftige Mauern und Wände auch raumbildend und dienen als Speichermasse. An der West- und Südfront bringen schlanke Stahlstützen und raumhohe Verglasungen das Bergpanorama optimal zur Geltung. Sowohl die Decke zwischen Unter- und Obergeschoß als auch die große Platte des Daches sind als Hohlkasten mit Furnierschichtholztafeln (Kerto) und Stegen aus Brettschichtholz konstruiert, sodass unüblich weite Auskragungen und Stützenabstände bewältigt werden können. Das geringe Gewicht und die Möglichkeit, die Wärmedämmung in der Deckenstärke zu integrieren, sprechen für Holz. Stichbalken tragen die Balkone; für die Roste und die Gartenterrasse kam das witterungsbeständige und fußfreundliche Holz der Tanne zum Zug. Eine sorgfältig konzipierte Entwässerung sorgt für lange Haltbarkeit.

The two-story residential building facing the valley lies at 720 meters above sea level on an old square overlooking the village. The view of the rocky, snow-peaked expanse of the Bregenzerwald Forest from the tree-lined southeastern mountain flank is virtually incomparable. The protruding, flat roof covers and provides shadow for two structures, an open zone in between and a balcony wrapped around the entire building. The smaller of the two buildings whose closed façade is the first thing seen by arriving visitors, contains a double garage on top and a sauna underneath. The wide zone in between with stairs down to the garden terrace creates the impression of a covered anteroom leading to the larger structure, which contains cooking, dining and living spaces as well as a studio on the upper level. The lower level contains the bedrooms and generously proportioned service areas. The site plan is structured as a set of layers constructed parallel to the progression of the slope: The flat balcony comes first, followed by the bedrooms with their three-way glass paneling. This is followed by the ancillary and sanitary facilities, and finally, in the back, lie the technical equipment rooms and cellars. These rooms are set below ground level, against the incline of the terrain. This alignment creates a longitudinal prismatic link between the two project parts. Towards the southwest, the balcony platform is over three meters deep and offers outside seating possibilities. In structural terms, the back area's powerful walls serve to delineate space and store heat. Slender steel struts are used on the west and south fronts as well as floor-to-ceiling glass paneling to do justice to the mountain panorama. Both the ceiling between the lower and upper level and the large roof slab are made of hollow, boxed-shaped structures featuring veneer timber cladding and bonded timber bridging elements. This made it possible to create uncommonly large projecting surfaces with broadly spaced struts. The low weight and the possibility of integrating heat insulation elements in the thickness of the roof spoke for the use of timber. Tail beams support the balconies. Fir timber, which is comfortable to walk on, was used for the gratings and garden terrace. A carefully conceived drainage system ensures longevity.

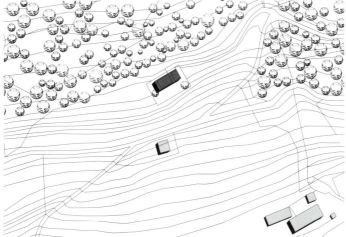

2001
Langen bei Bregenz, Austria
Bauherrschaft | Client: Reinhard Fuchs, Langen
Mitarbeit | Assistence: Martin Rümmele

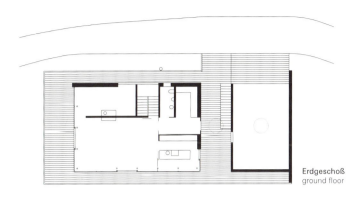

Erdgeschoß
ground floor

Untergeschoß
basement

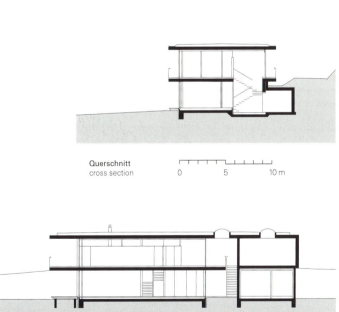

Querschnitt
cross section

Längsschnitt
longitudinal section

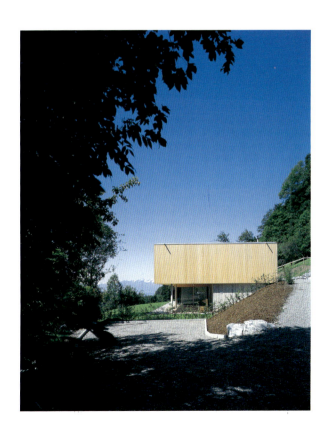

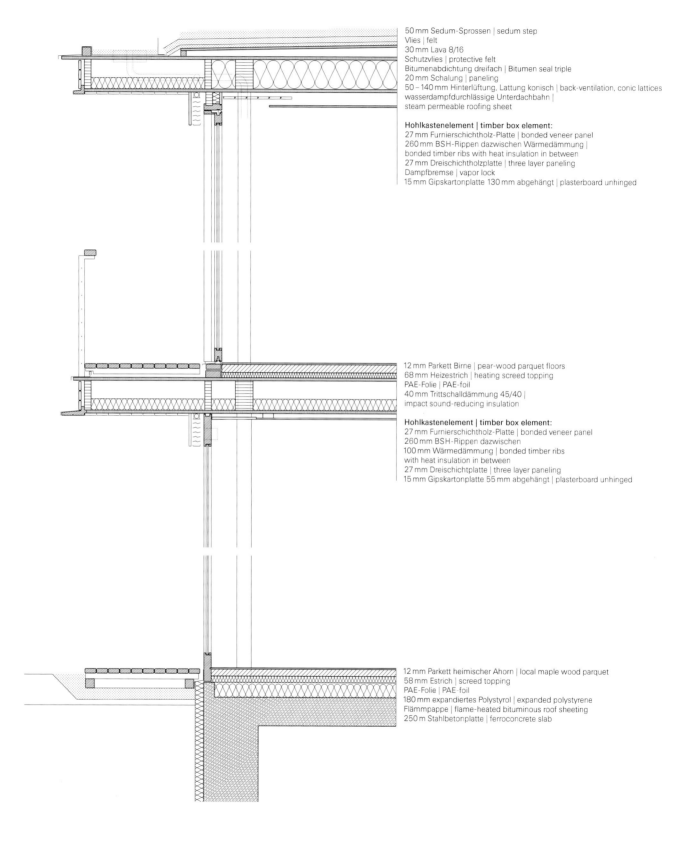

Christian Lenz

Haus Raid, Schwarzach
House Raid, Schwarzach

Das Backsteingebäude steht in der mit Einfamilienhäusern besetzten Entwicklungszone vergangener Jahrzehnte, wie sie in den Dörfern des Rheintals verbreitet sind. Das Satteldach, die strenge äußere Komposition mit raffiniert ausgewogenen Symmetrien und die Sichtziegelfassade lassen nicht sofort erkennen, dass die innere Organisation sich an modernen, fließenden Raumvorstellungen orientiert. Der von schmalhohen Fenstern in seiner Wirkung verstärkte Längstrakt und Hauptbaukörper wird quer von einer fragiler scheinenden Raumzone durchkreuzt, die sich offenbar gerade wegen ihrer Transparenz auf zwei Geschoßen zu behaupten vermag. Nach außen tritt sie mit dem Windfang im Norden und dem vorgebauten Speisezimmer im Süden in Erscheinung. Im Inneren sind es die Funktionen des Entrees, der Küche und des Essbereichs, die ihr Kontur verleihen. Gegenüber dem hohen Wohnraum auf der einen und den geschlossenen Nebenräumen und dem Schlafbereich auf der anderen Seite wird sie durch die klare Funktionszuschreibung ihrer Räume und Raumzonen akzentuiert. Im Obergeschoß konfrontieren sich der unbetretbare Luftraum über dem Wohnbereich und die dielenartigen Galerien, wobei letztere von elegant differenzierten Geländern geradezu nobilitiert werden. Den eingeschnürten Rest an Längsentwicklung bildet die Treppe. Wie ein Möbel steht sie mitten im Kreuzungsfeld und verbindet Geschoße und Hausteile in selbstverständlicher Weise. Den Innenausbau bestimmen Verfeinerung und Aufgliederung. Das reicht bis zur Verweigerung eines einzelnen Firstträgers im sichtbaren Dachgebälk, der aber den Raum unerwünscht scharf zerschnitten hätte. Dank Aufteilung und paarweiser Führung gewinnt die Raumzone der Treppe vertikale Konturen und durchkreuzt ihrerseits wieder den Raum. Alle diese konsequent durchgearbeiteten räumlichen Durchdringungen und Überlagerungen verleihen dem Bauwerk einen programmatischen Charakter. Dank der Italianità der gestalterischen Details ist es allerdings ein sehr wohnliches Manifest, das durch das vermeintlich „fremde" Element der Klinkersteine im Holzbauland so richtig geschärft wurde.

The redbrick building is located in an area that was developed decades ago, as was the case with many villages in the Rhine Valley, along with a number of single family houses. The saddle roof, the strict exterior composition with its refined symmetries and the open brick façade conceal the fact that the interior organization is based on modern, flowing room concepts. The tall, narrow windows emphasize the sense of length in the main building, which is traversed in its width by a fragile space whose transparency helps define it on two levels. This transparency is also conveyed by the porch facing north and the dining room projecting to the south. On the inside, it is the functions of offering an entrance space, the kitchen and the dining room areas that add contours to this sense of lightness. These contours are further accentuated by the clearly assigned functions in the other rooms and areas. This is evident in enclosed ancillary rooms and the bedroom area on the other side. On the upper level, the inaccessible open space above the living area is juxtaposed with the hall-like galleries, which are nobly enhanced by varying elegantly designed railings. The last element integrated in this impression of overall length is staircase at the intercestion of the housse that connects levels and areas with matter-of-fact efficiency. Refinement and organization define the interior. This includes avoiding the use of a single roof crest support, which would have cut the room in an undesirable manner. Thanks to its distribution and strucutre in pairs, the staricase area gains vertical contours and traverses the room itself. These thoroughly engineered spatial penetrations and layers give the building a programmatic character. However, the Italian air of the design details create a manifesto of living space that was actually honed by "foreign" brick element in an area defined by timber construction.

1988
Schwarzach, Austria
Bauherrschaft | Client: Othmar Raid, Schwarzach
Mitarbeit | Assistence: Elisabeth Rüdisser
Publikation | Publication: Häuser, 01/1994; Einfamilienhäuser aus Backstein,
Anton Graf, Callwey Verlag München, 1998; Baukunst in Vorarlberg seit 1980
Kunsthaus Bregenz, VAI, 1998

154 Einfamilienhäuser Single-Family Houses

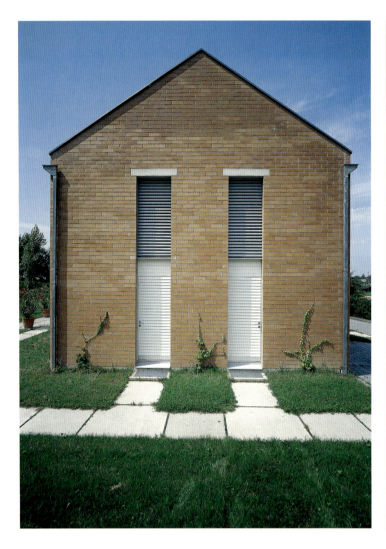

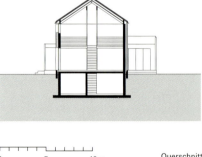

Querschnitt
cross section

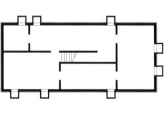
Untergeschoß
basement

Erdgeschoß
ground floor

Obergeschoß
upper floor

Christian Lenz

Doppelhaus Klosterwiesweg, Schwarzach

Two-family House Klosterwiesweg, Schwarzach

Die Erweiterung am Sportplatzweg im Dorfteil nördlich des Helbernbaches folgt einem siedlungsbaulichen Konzept von Manfred Türtscher. Das Doppelhaus befindet sich im Binnenbereich der Bebauungsstruktur. Am Zufahrtsweg steht ein breites Flugdach, das die Autos, die Hauszugänge und zwei daruntergestellte Geräteraum-Boxen beschirmt. Dahinter schließt der geometrisch klare, zweigeschoßige Quader an, der die beiden 4 1/2-Zimmer-Häuser mit je 90 Quadratmetern Nutzfläche enthält. Dem Entwurfsziel entsprechend, „eine flächenmäßig reduzierte Wohneinheit zu schaffen, die bei eingeschränkten finanziellen Möglichkeiten dennoch ein Wohnen im eigenen Garten" erlaubt, ist der Grundriss kompakt. Das Wohnen ist breit nach Süden orientiert, die nordseitig platzierte Küche verfügt über ein Ausblicksfenster zum Eingang. Die Sanitärräume und Treppen sind in dem vom Sonnenlauf weniger verwöhnten Grundrissteil konzentriert. Die Zimmer sind knapp, aber ausreichend dimensioniert. Parallel zu diesem sparsamen Grundrisskonzept diente das Doppelhaus als Pilotprojekt für eine vorgefertigte Bauweise aus Brettstapeltafeln und weiteren Holzwerkstoffen. Für den Fassadenschirm wurden hingegen schlanke Latten aus Lärchenholz verwendet. Außer der Kostenoptimierung erfuhr das Objekt jedoch eine gestalterische Zuwendung, die mit den klassischen Mitteln einfacher Architektur arbeitete: ausgewogene Proportionen sowie die sorgfältige und präzise Ordnung der notwendigen Elemente zu einem angemessenen und ansprechenden Ganzen. Dies beginnt bei der volumetrischen Gliederung von Vorhaus und Haupthaus, dem geschützten Weg zur Haustür und der architektonisch abgestuften Beziehung zum Garten. Es geht weiter mit der ausgewogenen Gartenfassade, den ruhigen Stirnseiten und einem freundlichen, das Konstruktionsmaterial Holz als Oberflächenmaterial nutzenden Innenausbau. Und es kulminiert beim Eckdetail der Schirmlatten an der Fassade, der exakten Platzierung der Regenrohre oder der elegant scharfen Dachkante. Architektonische Maßnahmen dieser Art und Qualität sind in dieser Preiskategorie üblicherweise nicht zu bekommen.

The expansion along the Sportplatzweg Path in the village section north of the Helbernbach Creek was completed according to a housing project concept devised by Manfred Türtscher. The two-family unit is located in the mid-section of the area zoned for construction. The driveway is covered by a wide canopy, that protects the cars, house entryways and to machinery sheds underneath. The geometrically clear, two-story square building lies directly behind the driveway/garage area. The structure contains both of the 4 1/2-room residential units, which feature 90 square meters of floor space. In accordance with the design objective of creating a residential unit with limited financial resources on a reduced space that would nonetheless allow tenants to, "live in their own gardens," the site plan is very compact. The living spaces are aligned to the south, with the kitchen facing north. It features a window that offers a view of the entrance. The sanitary rooms and steps are concentrated in the area that receives less sunlight. The rooms are compact, but offer sufficient space. In keeping with this cost-efficient floor plan concept, the two-family house also served as a pilot project for a prefabricated construction technique that makes use of composite timber cladding and other timber components. Slender larch lathes were used on the façade shielding. The building is defined by the cost-efficient construction method and the attention that was given to its design with the means of classical architecture: well-balanced proportions and the careful and precise organization of the necessary elements make the building a commensurate and appealing whole. This effect begins with the volumetric structure of the entrance hall and main house, the protected path to the house door and the architecturally composed relationship to the garden. The impression is also stressed by the balanced garden façade, the calm gable ends and the friendly interiors that make use of structural timber as a surface material. The effect is completed by the protective lathes applied to the façade as corner details, the exact placement of the rain gutters and the elegantly sharp roof ledge. Architectural touches of this form and quality aren't available in this form and quality in this price range normally.

1997
Schwarzach, Austria
Bauherrschaft | Client: Revital Bauträger GmbH, Dornbirn
Mitarbeit | Assistence: Helmut Brunner
Baukunst in Vorarlberg seit 1980, Kunsthaus Bregenz, VAI, 1998

Obergeschoß
upper floor

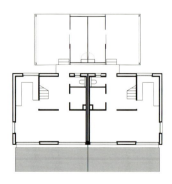
Erdgeschoß
ground floor

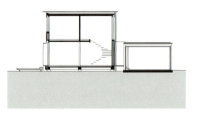
Querschnitt
cross section

0   5   10 m

Einfamilienhäuser — Single-Family Houses

Konstruktiv lagert das Doppelhaus auf Punktfundamenten (Piloten), auf denen pro Gebäudehälfte zwei Pfostenstapelelemente aufliegen. Der Zwischenraum zum Erdboden ist durchlüftet, eine zementgebundene Spanplatte schützt die kräftige Mineralwolledämmung. Als Brandschutzwand dienen Betonelemente verkleidet mit Pfostenstapelelementen. Für die tragenden Außenwände kamen mit Langspanplatten ausgesteifte Pfostenstapelelemente zum Einsatz. Davor liegt die von Konstruktionshölzern ungestörte Wärmedämmung. Geschoßdecken und Dach sind ebenfalls als Pfostenstapelelemente ausgebildet, zur Trittschalldämmung dienen Weichfaserplatten, die Hohlräume sind mit Mineralwolle gedämmt, als Oberfläche des Schiffbodens wurde Lärche gewählt. Dem kargen Ausbau steht eine hochwertige Wärmedämmung entgegen, sodass die Energiewerte einer ähnlich großen Geschoßwohnung eher noch unterschritten werden. Die gewonnenen Erfahrungen aus dem konsequent vorgefertigten Bauwerk gelangten unter anderem beim Apartmenthaus Lechblick zur Anwendung.

Structurally, the two-family house rests on foundation blocks, with two composite slabs under each half of the building. The space between these elements and the ground is ventilated, with bonded cement panel cladding to protect the effective mineral wool insulation. Cement elements featuring bonded wood paneling are used as fire-protection panels. Bonded timber cladding with stiffening composite lathes were used on the exterior supporting walls. The insulation elements lie directly in front, undisturbed by the structural timber. The floor ceilings and roof were also made of bonded timber panels using soft fiber boards to offer acoustic damping. The hollow spaces were filled with mineral wool and larch ship planking was used on the surface. The bleak exterior structure is counter-balanced by high-quality insulation, allowing the apartments to achieve lower energy consumption levels than other similarly large one-story apartments. The experience gleaned from this rigorous experiment with prefabricated building techniques was applied to the Lechblick Apartment building, among others.

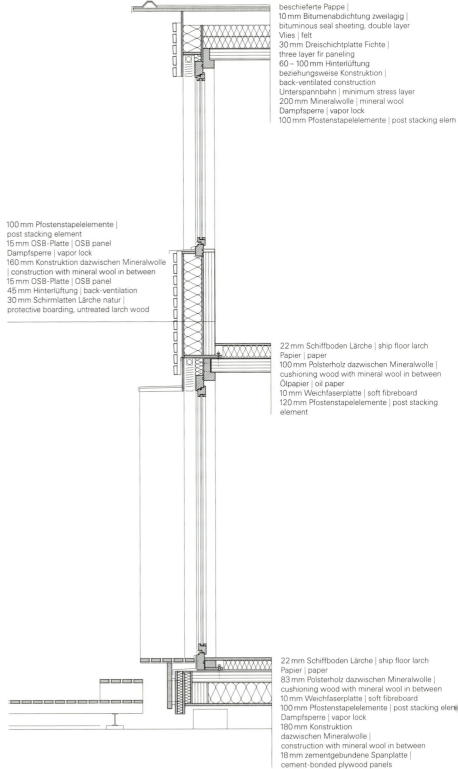

beschieferte Pappe |
10 mm Bitumenabdichtung zweilagig | bituminous seal sheeting, double layer
Vlies | felt
30 mm Dreischichtplatte Fichte | three layer fir paneling
60 – 100 mm Hinterlüftung beziehungsweise Konstruktion | back-ventilated construction
Unterspannbahn | minimum stress layer
200 mm Mineralwolle | mineral wool
Dampfsperre | vapor lock
100 mm Pfostenstapelelemente | post stacking elem

100 mm Pfostenstapelelemente | post stacking element
15 mm OSB-Platte | OSB panel
Dampfsperre | vapor lock
160 mm Konstruktion dazwischen Mineralwolle | construction with mineral wool in between
15 mm OSB-Platte | OSB panel
45 mm Hinterlüftung | back-ventilation
30 mm Schirmlatten Lärche natur | protective boarding, untreated larch wood

22 mm Schiffboden Lärche | ship floor larch
Papier | paper
100 mm Polsterholz dazwischen Mineralwolle | cushioning wood with mineral wool in between
Ölpapier | oil paper
10 mm Weichfaserplatte | soft fibreboard
120 mm Pfostenstapelelemente | post stacking element

22 mm Schiffboden Lärche | ship floor larch
Papier | paper
83 mm Polsterholz dazwischen Mineralwolle | cushioning wood with mineral wool in between
10 mm Weichfaserplatte | soft fibreboard
100 mm Pfostenstapelelemente | post stacking elem
Dampfsperre | vapor lock
180 mm Konstruktion dazwischen Mineralwolle | construction with mineral wool in between
18 mm zementgebundene Spanplatte | cement-bonded plywood panels

Christian Lenz

Haus Lenz, Schwarzach

House Lenz, Schwarzach

Das elegante Haus befindet sich am südlichen Rand des Dorfes, wo sich bis vor wenigen Jahren noch Obstgärten ausbreiteten, die teilweise noch heute das Landschaftsbild mitbestimmen. Das lang gezogene Bauwerk ist breit nach Süden geöffnet, während die Fassade nach Norden dank eines langen Bandfensters im Obergeschoß nicht unfreundlich wirkt, aber ansonsten doch mehrheitlich geschlossen ist. Ein eingeschoßiger Baukörper mit Garage und Geräteraum definiert einen Vorplatz, wobei der Lattenschild der geschlossenen Garagentore unmissverständlich zum Hauseingang hinweist. Am Hauptbaukörper ist das Thema „massiver Sockel und leichter Oberbau" exemplarisch ausgeführt: Den exakt gearbeiteten Sichtbetonsockel trennt ein schmales Oberlichtband vom holzverschalten Oberbau, der somit abgehoben erscheint, ohne dass tragende Elemente offensichtlich wären. Die architektonische Unterscheidung zwischen massivem Erdgeschoß und leicht gebautem, „schwebendem" Obergeschoß könnte kaum deutlicher sein. Der auf den ersten Blick exakt geometrische Baukörper weist an drei Seiten eingeschnittene Außenräume auf, die, entsprechend ihrer Ausrichtung, Variationen des Außenwohnens übernehmen. Nach Osten, mit direkter Beziehung zur Küche, bietet eine große Gartenplattform Platz für ein sonniges Frühstück oder ein schattiges Mittagessen. An der Stirnseite nach Westen weist das Obergeschoß eine Loggia auf zum gemütlichen Sitzen nach Feierabend. Nach Süden sind Schlafzimmer und zugeordnete Sanitärräume hinter einen flachen Balkon zurückgezogen, beschattet von der rahmenartig ausgeschnittenen Gebäudehülle. Das Innere des schlanken Grundrisses weist im Norden einen schmalen Streifen mit Wirtschaftsraum, Entree, Treppe und Gang, WC sowie einem kleinen Büro auf, während die Südseite von einer breiten Raumfolge aus Küche, Essen, Wohnen und Bibliothek beansprucht wird. Der von einer Doppelstütze fein zonierte Wohnbereich ist somit U-förmig von funktional eindeutig bestimmten Räumen umfangen. Sie bilden gleichsam einen räumlichen Puffer für den weniger klar definierten, funktional weichen Kern „Wohnen".

The elegant house is located on the southern edge of the village, which was the site of a number of orchards, which still define the landscape until a few years ago. The long structure opens wide to the south, while the northern façade makes a friendly impression thanks to the long ribbon of windows on the upper level, although it is largely enclosed. A one-story structure including a garage and tool shed defines a forecourt with the lathes of the closed garage doors acting as an unmistakable sign post to the houses' entrance. The main structure is an exemplary sample of the "solid base course and light upper structure" theme. The precisely engineered unfinished cement base course is separated from the timber-clad upper section by a small transom. Thus the upper level seems to hover over the bottom section without any apparent supporting elements. The architectural differentiation between the massive ground level and the "hovering," lightly structured upper level couldn't be more clearly achieved. At first glance, the building seems to be defined by exact geometry, however, this impression is disturbed by incisions that create additional outer living space on three sides of the building. These spaces can be used for various outdoor living activities and in accordance to the points they lie on. To the east, directly linked to the kitchen, lies a large garden platform that can be used for a breakfast in the sun or lunch in the shadows. On the gable end, the upper level features a loggia for a comfortable evening at home after work. The bedrooms and corresponding sanitary facilities are aligned facing south and recessed behind a flat balcony. Shadow is provided by the frame-like incisions of the building shell. The interior of the slim grounds plan features a narrow strip that houses the service room, entrance, steps and WC, as well as a small office facing north. The south side comprises a sequence of wider rooms including the kitchen, dining room, living room and library. The living room are is elegantly zoned by a double strut and thus clearly defined functional rooms surround this space in a U-shaped pattern. This arrangement creates a spatial buffer for the more ambiguously defined, functionally soft, "living" core.

1996
Schwarzach, Austria
Bauherrschaft | Client: Birgit und Christian Lenz, Schwarzach
Publikation | Publication: Der Standard, 25.10.2000
Baukunst in Vorarlberg seit 1980, Kunsthaus Bregenz, VAI, 1998

Querschnitt
cross section

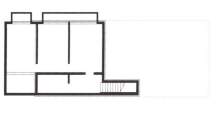

Untergeschoß
basement

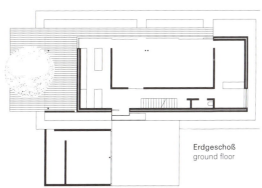

Erdgeschoß
ground floor

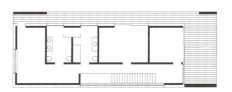

Obergeschoß
upper floor

Christian Lenz

Haus Hagspiel, Höchst

House Hagspiel, Höchst

Das Grundstück, ein ehemaliger Obstgarten im sehr locker bebauten westlichen Dorfteil, hat einen unüblich lang gestreckten, polygonalen Zuschnitt. Der Entwurf reagiert darauf mit einem extrem schlanken Baukörper im Binnenbereich des Gevierts. Die Zufahrt erfolgt über eine kurze Stichgasse von Norden her. Das reine Weiß und die ebenso reine Geometrie des Bauwerks heben es aus der Umgebung heraus und verstärken den Effekt autonomer Ganzheit. Diesen Eindruck vermögen die südseitig herausgezogenen Funktionen Esszimmer und Küche, die sich hinter einer holzverschalten Schirmwand verbergen, nicht zu relativieren. Lange Bandfenster, raumhohe Glaswände und einzelne kleine Lochfenster sind zwar mit Bezug zu den dahinterliegenden Funktionen, aber doch so auf der Fassade verteilt, dass diese in einen ausbalancierten Spannungszustand versetzt wird, der in der Mitte eine starke Dehnung erfährt. Der Anteil an geschlossener Mauerfläche wächst zu den Gebäudekanten hin an. So vermögen diese das heftige Kräftespiel der Öffnungen, deren Formate und Proportionen gleich einer optischen Klammer zusammenzuhalten. Dabei spielt der Raumdurchschuss im vorderen Teil des Hauses, der dem Abstellen des Autos dient, eine eigene Rolle. Anders als die flächig verglasten Fenster betont er den körperhaften Charakter des Bauwerks. Im stark gestreckten Grundriss kommt die Treppe in die Mitte zu liegen, jeweils zusammen mit einem dielenartigen Raum, der als Verteiler fungiert. Im Erdgeschoß hat er zugleich die Funktion des Esszimmers. Die Länge des Grundrisses bringt es mit sich, dass in diesem Haus im positiven Sinn merkbare innere Distanzen existieren, und obwohl die Räume im gegebenen Volumen verbleiben, gewinnen sie allein aus der Extremposition beziehungsweise aus einer unbestrittenen Mittellage ihre spezifische Individualität und Identität. Was einmal aus der Not des schmalen Grundrisses begonnen wurde, erinnert als fertiges Bauwerk in keiner Weise mehr an äußere Zwänge, und es scheint, als hätten die Grundstücksgrenzen nicht bestanden.

The site, a former orchard in the very sparsely developed western part of the village is defined by its unusually long polygon-like shape. The designer reacted to this feature by creating an extremely slim structure in the inner space of the area. Access is possible via a short alley to the north. The pure white color and pure geometry of the structure set it apart from the surroundings and emphasize the impression of autonomous completeness. This impression is not relativized by the functional dining room and kitchen hidden behind a timber-clad screen wall projecting from the southern side of the building. Long ribbons of windows, floor-to-ceiling glass panels and individual bull's eyes that indicate the function of the rooms behind them are distributed across the façade in a way that convey a sense of well-balanced architectural tension that is markedly stretched in the building's mid-section. The amount of enclosed wall surfaces increases towards the edges of the building, thus providing a visual bracket for the considerable tension between the openings, their forms and their proportions. The spatial grid of the houses' front section, which serves as the parking lot plays its own role in this design. As opposed to the large glass window surfaces, the parking lot stresses the corporeal aspects of the building. The extremely long floor plan placed the steps in the middle together with a hall-like room that serves as a distribution point. On the ground level, it also acts as the dining room. The length of the site plan allows distance to be perceived as a positive feature in this building. This extreme placement makes it possible for the rooms to develop their specific individuality and identity, although they were built with the given volume. What began as a necessity due to the narrow grounds plan The completed building does not remind the visitor in anyway of the fact that its was the result of the necessities dictated by the narrow grounds plan and its almost seems as if the borders of the plot had never existed.

1995
Höchst, Austria
Bauherrschaft | Client: Edith und Karl Hagspiel, Höchst
Mitarbeit | Assistence: Gernot Bösch
Publikation | Publication: Baukunst in Vorarlberg seit 1980,
Kunsthaus Bregenz, VAI, 1998

Obergeschoß
upper floor

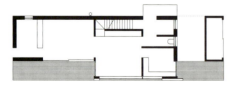

Erdgeschoß
ground floor

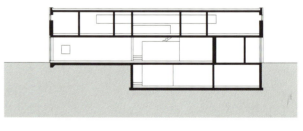

Längsschnitt
longitudinal section

0   5   10 m

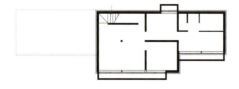

Untergeschoß
basement

Einfamilienhäuser Single-Family Houses

Christian Lenz

Haus Eggler, Wolfurt

House Eggler, Wolfurt

Der von Bachtälern fingerartig gefurchte Hang oberhalb des langen Straßendorfes fällt nach Westen ab, das Grundstück befindet sich in einer muldenartigen Geländefalte, die im Süden von einer locker bewaldeten Kante begrenzt wird. Seit Jahrzehnten stehen dort verschiedenste Häuser. Der Neubau präsentiert sich als breiter, massiver Stahlbetonrahmen, der bergseitig mit einer Kante aufliegt und sich talseitig gleichsam „en passant" einem schlanken Stahlstützenpaar anvertraut. Darunter bleibt Raum für einen teils offenen, teils als Gartenhalle verglasten Sitzplatz. Die zwei Geschoße in dem von Rahmen gefassten Hauptbaukörper sind nach Süden, zum terrassierten Garten, weit geöffnet. Nach Norden ist der Rahmen flächig mit hinterlüfteten Eternittafeln gefüllt, in die kleine Fenster gleichen Querformats geschnitten sind. Der natürliche Terrainverlauf lässt hier den Baukörper stärker aus dem Hang heraustreten, sodass die Rückseite die tragende Idee des aus dem Hang strebenden volumetrischen Konzepts zeigt. Die nach Westen gerichtete Stirnseite ist geschlossen bis auf eine breite Ausblicksöffnung im obersten Geschoß. Sie gehört zur söllerartigen Loggia, die dem großen Wohnraum vorgelagert ist. Damit nützt das Wohngeschoß mit Küche, Essplatz-Wohnen und einem nordseitigen Arbeitsraum die Höhenlage für die bis hin zum See reichende Aussicht. Das Schlafgeschoß befindet sich darunter im Eingangsgeschoß, aus dessen Halle sich die verbindende Treppe großzügig nach oben entwickelt. Seinen eleganten Charakter verdankt das Gebäude den zusammenfassenden, exakt gegossenen, gedämmten Stahlbetonplatten, die mit den seitlichen Betonscheiben zu einem bildhaften Rahmen verbunden sind. Dazu im Kontrast sind die Steher der raumhohen Glaswände und Schiebefenster viel schlanker proportioniert, während die zarten Stahlstützen optisch soweit ausgeblendet werden, dass sie räumlich unwirksam sind und kaum als konstruktive Elemente wahrgenommen werden. Der Ertrag dieser gestalterischen Maßnahmen sind offene und luftige Räume, die den Luxus der Weite zelebrieren, die von der Aussicht ins Haus geholt wird.

The slope of above the streets of the winding village is etched with finger-like creek valleys and drops off to the west. The site is located in a depression along a fault in the terrain that is bordered by a loosely afforested edge of woodland on the south. Various houses have stood there for decades. The new building is a wide, massive ferroconcrete framework structure resting on the mountain side at an angle while casually relying on the support of a pair of slender steel stays. Underneath there is space for a partially open, partially glass paneled seating area. The two levels of the main building defined by the framework open wide, facing the terraced garden to the south. The frame features large surfaces furnished with back-ventilated Eternit panels with identical small elongated rectangular windows cut into them. The natural course of the terrain allows the building to project from the slope more forcefully, which in turn emphasizes the volumetric concept and intention of creating a building that seems to break out of the slope. The gable end faces west and is closed, except for a large opening offering a panoramic view on the uppermost level. It belongs to the attic-like loggia that is located in front of the large living room area. Thus this level makes use of its elevation to provide the kitchen, dining room and living room an view that includes the lake. The bedroom level is on the ground floor that features a generously dimensioned flight of connecting steps that takes visitors to the upper level. The building owes its elegant character to the precisely cast and the insulated ferroconcrete slabs that create a graphically vivid frame for the buildings along with the lateral cement panels. The beams in the ceiling-to-floor glass paneled rooms and the sliding glass doors offer a stark contrast with their much slender proportions. The slim stays are so visually unobtrusive that they achieve no spatial effect and are not registered as structural elements. The fruits of these design measures are open, airy rooms that celebrate the luxury of the far reaches the houses' view has to offer.

1998
Wolfurt, Austria
Bauherrschaft | Client: Brigitte und Andreas Eggler, Wolfurt
Mitarbeit | Assistence: Jürgen Erath
Publikation | Publication: Der Standard, 25.09.1999;
Beton Zement 02/99

Single-Family Houses

Obergeschoß
upper floor

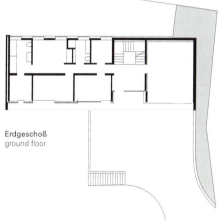

Erdgeschoß
ground floor

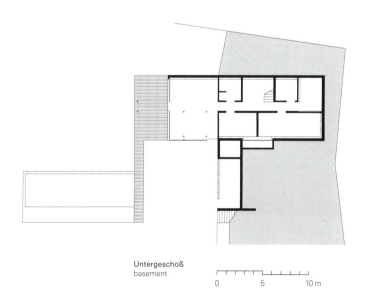

Untergeschoß
basement

0 5 10 m

Querschnitt
cross section

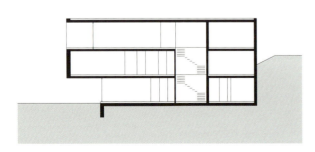

Längsschnitt
longitudinal section

175 Einfamilienhäuser — Single-Family Houses

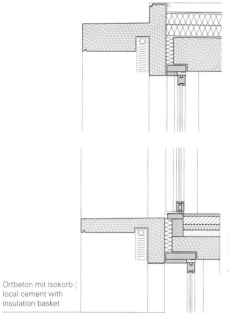

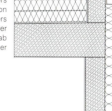

50 mm Kies | grave 16/32
Bitumenbahn zweilagig | bitumen roofing sheet, two layers
200 mm Wärmedämmung | heat insulation
Bitumenbahn einlagig | bitumen roofing sheet, one layers
Voranstrich | preliminary layer
250–300 mm Stahlbetonplatte | ferroconcrete slab
10 mm Putz glatt | smooth plaster

22 mm Parkett | parquet
70 mm Estrich | screed topping
Folie | foil
50 mm Wärmedämmung | heat insulation
58 mm Dämmschüttung | insulation filling
250 mm Stahlbetonplatte | ferroconcrete slab
10 mm Putz glatt | smooth plaster

Ortbeton mit Isokorb |
local cement with
insulation basket

12 mm Zementfaserplatte | cement fiberboard
30/50 mm Lattung/Hinterlüftung | lathes/back-ventilation
160 mm Wärmedämmung | heat insulation
180 mm Mauerwerk | walls
10 mm Putz glatt | smooth plaster

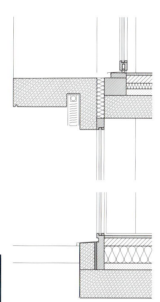

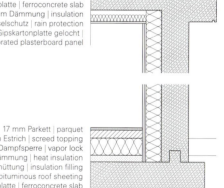

22 mm Parkett | parquet
70 mm Estrich | screed topping
50 mm Folie | foil
58 mm Dämmschüttung
250 mm Stahlbetonplatte | ferroconcrete slab
60 mm Dämmung | insulation
Rieselschutz | rain protection
15 mm Gipskartonplatte gelocht |
perforated plasterboard panel

17 mm Parkett | parquet
70 mm Estrich | screed topping
Dampfsperre | vapor lock
150 mm Wärmedämmung | heat insulation
58 mm Dämmschüttung | insulation filling
Flämmpappe | flame-heated bituminous roof sheeting
250 mm Stahlbetonplatte | ferroconcrete slab

Christian Lenz

Zubau Hallenbad Hampl, Lochau

Hampl Indoor Swimming Pool Annex, Lochau

Das Haus am westexponierten Hang über der Lochauer Bucht hatte Wolfgang Ritsch entworfen. Der disziplinierten Vorarlberger Baukunst konnte Jahre später ein im Ausdruck unabhängig konzipierter Raum hinzugefügt werden. Während das ältere Satteldachhaus parallel den Höhenlinien folgt, steht der Neubauteil orthogonal dazu, sodass der niedrige Baukörper bergseitig in den Hang eingesenkt ist. Seine Stirne tritt aus dem Terrain heraus. Sie gewinnt damit Autonomie, die vom querformatigen Ausblicksfenster unterstrichen wird. Eine Terrasse, die in das flache Dach über der Schwimmhalle übergeht, vermittelt zwischen Bestand und Neubau. Dessen Gebäudeschale aus Sichtbeton weist mehrere Öffnungen auf, die das Einfangen des Tageslichts und die Ausblicke steuern. Die frühe Sonne gelangt mit ihren Strahlen von hinten durch das zweiflächige Fenster in der südlichen Dachkante und bestreicht kurz die Wand aus Osttiroler Kalkstein. Als Mittagssonne fällt sie steil ins Schwimmbecken ein und evoziert eine Diagonale in die rechtwinkelige Raumstruktur, während sie am Nachmittag immer flacher durch das breite Westfenster eindringt. An Sommerabenden erreicht sie die Glasschiebewände im Norden, die den Schwimmbereich zur unteren Terrassenplattform öffnen. Von innen gesehen exponiert das hochliegende Dachkantenfenster Baumwipfel und Himmel, die stirnseitige Öffnung rahmt die Aussicht auf den See, während die Glaswände zur Terrasse den Raum aufreißen, sodass das fraktionierte Panorama bis zum benachbarten Lindau reicht. Die Grenzfläche zwischen Luft und Wasser als virtuelle Fortsetzung des Fußbodens zaubert den Himmel auf den Beckenspiegel. Auch wenn die Natursteinwand durchgeht, ist den Menschen die Welt darunter nur kurz zugänglich. Insgesamt wirkt der Raum weder bergend noch einschließend, sondern dramatisch geöffnet, sodass er als verdichtete Zone des unendlichen Raumes aufzufassen ist. Typologisch wirkt er in seiner materialen Konkretisierung aus Naturstein und Beton wie ein archaischer Unterstand, gleichsam analog zu der uralten Kulturtechnik des Bewegens an der Grenze von Wasser und Luft.

The building on a site that is exposed to the west on the slope overlooking the Lochau bay was built by Wolfgang Ritsch. An independently conceived space was added to the building, which is a sample of disciplined Vorarlberg architecture. Whereas the old, double-pitch roof follows the elevation lines parallel to it, the new building lies in an orthogonal direction. Hence the lower structure is imbedded in the slope. The narrow ends project beyond the edges of the terrain. The sense of autonomy is stressed by the broad panoramic windows. A terrace which continues as the mono-pitch roof of the swimming hall reconciles the existing building with the new annex. The unfinished cement shell thereof features a number of openings that coordinate the flow of light and the views. The early morning sun rays stream into the building through the double layer of windows at the back on the southern edge of the roof and briefly caress the walls made of East Tyrolean limestone walls. By midday, the sun falls on the swimming pool at a steep angle before streaming into the building at a flatter angle via the wide western window in the afternoon. During summer evenings, light enters the building the sliding glass walls to the north, which open the swimming area towards the the lower platform level. From the inside, the high roof edge window exposes tree crowns and the sky, while the opening on the narrow end frames the view of the lake. The glass walls facing the terrace open the room, allowing for the fractious view to be extended to include the neighboring town of Lindau. The bordering zones composed by the air and water function as a virtual continuation of the floor with the sky reflecting on the surface of the pool. The world below is only accesible for a moment due to the contiuous natural stone wall. hence the room is neither enclosing nor constricting, instead, it opens dramatically. This make it more of a dense zone within an infinite space. Typologically, it seems to be an archaic shelter with its natural stone and cement components, and it is analogous to the age-old cultural challenge of moving on the edge between water and air.

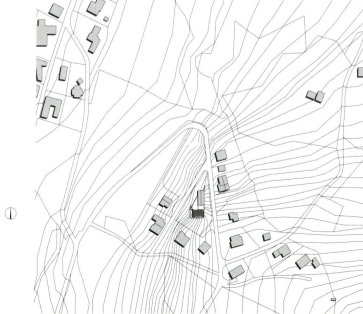

2001
Lochau, Austria
Bauherrschaft | Client: Margit und Peter Hampl, Lochau
Statik | Structural engineering: Mader & Flatz
Ziviltechniker GmbH, Bregenz
Mitarbeit | Assistence: Helmut Brunner

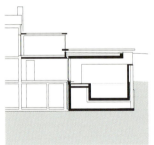
Querschnitt
cross section

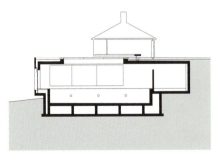
Längsschnitt
longitudinal section

0   5   10 m

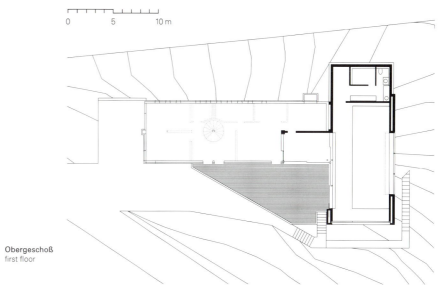

Obergeschoß
first floor

180 Einfamilienhäuser   Single-Family Houses

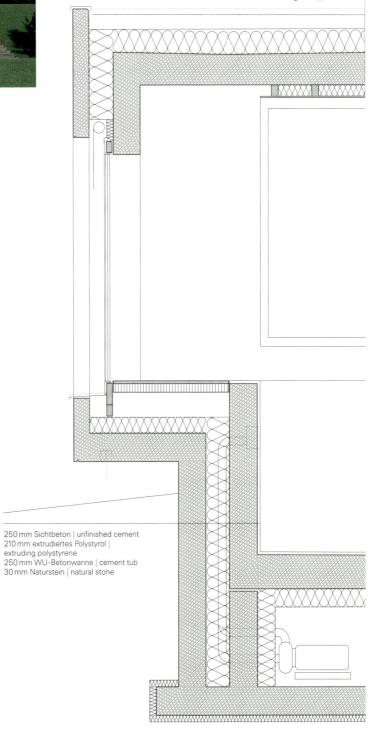

120 mm extensive Begrünung | extensive greenery
Foliendach | foil roofing
180 mm Wärmedämmung | heat insulation
Dachpappe einlagig | roofing sheet, one layer
270 mm Beton | cement
Hera-Flachs | Hera-Flax
Rieselschutzfolie | rain protection foil
12 mm Sperrholzplatte beitseitig furniert | chipboard panel two sided veneer
Lochung 8/18 | perforation

250 mm Sichtbeton | unfinished cement
210 mm extrudiertes Polystyrol | extruding polystyrene
250 mm WU-Betonwanne | cement tub
30 mm Naturstein | natural stone

Erneuerungen

Refurbishments

Hermann Kaufmann

Gasthof Adler, Schwarzenberg

Restaurant Adler, Schwarzenberg

Der Ortskern von Schwarzenberg umfasst einen gut erhaltenen Dorfplatz, der von Kirche und Kirchhofmauer, einem Tanzhaus sowie vier mit Tiernamen bezeichneten Gasthäusern: Schäfle, Hirschen, Adler und Ochsen, räumlich definiert wird. Die wichtigen gesellschaftlichen Funktionen dieser Gebäude weisen den Ort als ländliche Agora aus, wo Angelegenheiten der Dorfgemeinschaft gelebt und verhandelt wurden. Seither hat sich der hier unverzichtbare Automobilverkehr des Außenraums bemächtigt. Mit der Erneuerung des Gasthaus Adler, dessen platzwirksame Blockwandfassade mit aufgefrischter Bemalung und erneuerten Fenstern in traditioneller Bauweise von bauphysikalisch überraschend guter Qualität nun wieder optimal zur Geltung gelangt, wurde jedoch ein kulturelles Lebenszeichen gesetzt. Das Innere des 1756 errichteten, 1865 umgebauten und im 20. Jahrhundert stark veränderten Gebäudes enthielt wenig historische Substanz. Das Sanierungskonzept für das zu einem anerkannten Speiserestaurant avancierte Haus bewahrte zwar die Struktur mit dem breiten axialen Gang, für eine pflegende Behandlung kam jedoch nur mehr die Stube, der Gastraum in der vorderen Gebäudeecke mit Ofen und Kredenz in Frage. Die anschließenden Spreiseräume wurden unter Wahrung von Proportionen, Maßstab und Material mit schlichtem Fichtenholz neu gestaltet. Der Detailentwurf reduzierte die Profilierung der Vertäfelungen und kombinierte historisches Mobiliar mit zeitgenössischen und zeitlosen Stücken, beispielsweise Bugholzsesseln. Eine versenkbare Wand teilt den kleinen Saal in zwei Speisezimmer, und eine Glaswand öffnet den Schankraum zum Gang. Hohlräume in den Leichtbauwänden enthalten die Kanäle für die Abluft, die unter der Decke abgesogen wird. Zuluft wird unter den Bänken eingeblasen. Neue Raumteilung und Oberflächen folgen der Struktur und der Materialität des Hauses und lassen dem Bestand den Vorrang. In angemessener Weise wird aus Alt und Neu eine unaufdringlich zeitgenössische Atmosphäre geschaffen, die Bewahren und Fortschreiten gleichermaßen enthält und einem nächsten Zeitschnitt gegenüber offen bleibt.

The center of Schwarzenberg comprises a well-maintained village square whose space is defined by church and churchyard walls, a dancing hall and four inns that bear the names of animals: Schäfle, Hirschen, Adler and Ochsen, (Sheep, Buck, Eagle and Ox) that surround it. The important social functions of these buildings define the area as the location for village assemblies at which village matters were lived and negotiated. Since then, the traffic no place can do without has taken over the outer spaces. The renovation of the Gasthaus Adler Inn, whose block wall façade with with refreshed painting and windows renovated in traditional style, which nonetheless gives them outstanding structural qualities helped heightens the building's appeal and was a signal for new cultural life. The interior of the building, which was built in 1756, refurbished in 1865 and signficantly changed in the 20th century was of little historical value. The renovation concept for the building which had been well-known for its restaurant preserved the structure with its wide axial hall, but the only other things treated carefully were the parlor in the front corner of the building along with the sideboard and furnace. The connecting dining rooms are new designs that were made with fir timber in keeping with the proper proportions and scale. The details reduced paneling mass and combined historical furniture with contemporary and timeless pieces, such as bent wood chairs. A retractable wall divides the small hall into two dining rooms and a glass wall opens towards the hall of the tap room. Hollow spaces in the lightweight walls contain ventilation channels for the air sucked in from under the ceiling. Fresh air is pumped in under the benches. The new spatial distribution and surfaces are in keeping with the materials of the building and give the existing older structure priority. An unobtrusive contemporary atmosphere was fashioned between old and new elements here that suggests both preservation and progress and remains open to the times to come.

1991
Schwarzenberg, Austria
Bauherrschaft | Client: Heidi und Engelbert Kaufmann, Schwarzenberg
Mitarbeit | Assistence: Gerold Leuprecht
Publikation | Publication: baumeister, Themenmagazin Sanierung, 04/1996
Gastlich Bauen, Prospekt

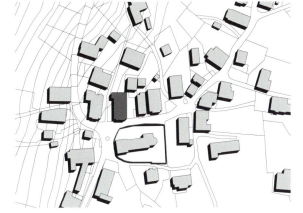

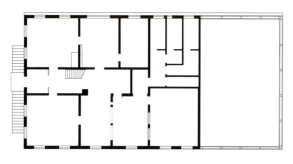

Erdgeschoß alt
ground floor old

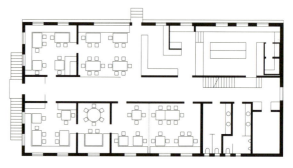

Erdgeschoß neu
ground floor new

Hermann Kaufmann

Haus Geissler, Wolfurt

House Geissler, Wolfurt

Die historische Dorfstruktur von Wolfurt zeigt in Teilen noch den Charakter des Straßendorfes, wo die dem Verkehr dienenden Außenräume durch kleinere, oft aber markante Zäsuren geprägt werden. Dies verleiht den öffentlichen Räumen spezifischen Reiz. Das ehemalige Bauernhaus Hofsteigstraße 1 grenzt mit dem Giebel an die Straße und bildet ein für den Verkehr im positiven Sinn verlangsamendes Engnis kurz vor einer wichtigen Abzweigung. Seine klare Position verbessert außer dem öffentlichen Raum auch die Orientierbarkeit im Ablauf der Dorfstraße. Obwohl die überalterte Substanz nicht erneuerbar war, konnte im gegebenen Volumen der Wohnteil neu errichtet werden. Auf dem Sockel des straßenseitig befindlichen Kellers erhebt sich ein Holzelementbau mit Brettstapeldecken. Ein großes Satteldach zieht sich gleichermaßen über den Neubau und den ehemals landwirtschaftlich genutzten alten Hausteil. Mit einer einfachen äußeren Form und einer unkomplizierten Grundrissaufteilung folgt der Entwurf sowohl traditionalen als auch zeitgenössischen Mustern. So wirkt die horizontale Fassadengliederung nach Geschoßen vertraut. Mit der auf die Innenräume bezogenen Fensterverteilung und den Schiebeläden werden jedoch moderne Prinzipien eingeführt. Das Gebäude wird damit datierbar. Die äußerste Schicht in eleganter Rhombenschalung aus schlanken Leisten ist sowohl irgendwie vertraut als auch zeitgenössisch – in der Anmutung einem Schindelschirm vergleichbar, aber eben doch anders. Dieser souveräne gestalterische Umgang mit konstruktiven und formalen Elementen führt zu zurückhaltender Ausgewogenheit, die für die Bebauungsstruktur und im Zusammenwirken mit den Nachbarbauten Gewinnbringend ist. Sie unterscheidet das Bauwerk von peinlich-schwülstigen Kompromissen und beziehungslos inszenierten Gegensätzen. Der Dialog über die Zeiten reicht bis zu den Details: ob dies nun das Regenrohr ist, das so nebenbei die Grenze von Alt und Neu markiert, oder die alte Türe, die, noch gebrauchsfähig, in den neuen Rahmen eingesetzt wurde, sodass der komplexe Prozess von Erneuern und Bewahren ablesbar bleibt.

The historical structure of the village of Wolfurt still shows the characteristics of a one-street village in which the outer spaces that are used for traffic are defined by a series of marked caesuras. This gives the public spaces their specific charm. The gable end of the former farm house at Hofsteigstraße 1 faces the street, creating a narrow bottleneck that slows traffic in a positive sense before it reaches an important crossing. Aside from upgrading this public space, its clear position also improves orientation as the village road runs it course. Although the aged original building could not be renovated, it was possible to refurbish the existing residential space. A timber component building with a bonded timber roof was set atop the base course of the cellar, which faces the street. A large double-pitch roof covers both the new section and the former farming section of the old structure. The simple exterior form and the uncomplicated grounds plan distribution of the design follows both traditional and contemporary patterns. Hence the horizontal façade organization by stories is familiar. However, the arrangement of the windows in correspondence with the rooms inside and their sliding components indicate the introduction of more modern principles, making it possible to date the building. The outermost layer is elegantly covered with elegant prism shaped boarding made of slender lattice work seems both familiar and contemporary – comparable to a shingle screen, but nonetheless different. This assured use of structural and formal elements leads to an impression of balanced restraint that is advantageous for both the new building and the overall structural composition along with the neighboring houses. This restraint sets it apart from the embarrasingly over-laden objects whose design lacks a sense of context. The dialogue of the varying eras even affects the details: whether it be the rain gutter that marks the border between old an new, or the old door that was set in a new frame since it could still be used. Hence the complex process of renewal and maintenance remains verifiable.

1999
Wolfurt, Austria
Bauherrschaft | Client: Familie Geissler, Wolfurt
Mitarbeit | Assistence: Peter Nussbaumer

Obergeschoß
upper floor

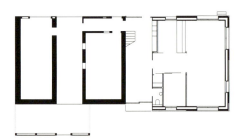

Erdgeschoß
ground floor

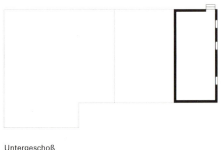

Untergeschoß
basement

0   5   10 m

Erneuerungen — Refurbishments

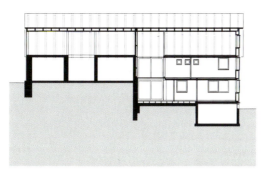

Längsschnitt
longitudinal section

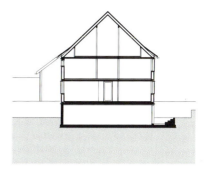

Querschnitt
cross section

Hermann Kaufmann, Christian Lenz, Helmut Dietrich, Wolfgang Ritsch

Fachhochschule Vorarlberg, Dornbirn

University of Applied Sciences, Dornbirn

Die städtebauliche Gliederung der prominent nach der Brücke über die Dornbirner Ach situierten, 1958 als Bundestextilschule von German Meusburger und Willi Ramersdorfer errichteten Anlage ist von stupender Eleganz. Das Volumen der Aula setzt an der Straße einen keck anschwingenden Auftakt. Daran schließt schmalhoch ein einhüftiger Klassentrakt an, auf den niedriger und breiter der wegscherende zweite, doppelbündige Klassentrakt anwortet. Eine verbindende Eingangshalle, die auch die rückwärtig gelegene ehemalige Wirkerei erschließt, öffnet sich auf den Gartenhof am Fluss. Der kleine, aufgestelzte Neubau über der südöstlich platzierten Tiefgarage fügt sich unauffällig in das Gesamtkonzept. Bauphysikalisch und hinsichtlich konstruktiver Details waren die fünfziger Jahre allerdings eine leichtlebige Zeit. Als daher 1981 die Textilschule geschlossen wurde, blieb das Bauwerk leer und galt als Ruine. Stadt und Bundesland ließen sich aber von engagierten Architekten und Stadtplanern von dessen Qualität überzeugen, sodass das Vorarlberger Hauptwerk der fünfziger Jahre nicht abgebrochen, sondern nach einer Sanierung der neuen Fachhochschule dient. Denkmalpflegerische Ansprüche und Erfahrungen sind für Bauten dieser Zeit noch rar. Der Ersatz der Fenster durch einen von den vier Architekten gemeinsam entwickelten Typ, der trotz Isolierverglasung nur geringfügig breitere Profile zeigt, wahrte den prinzipiellen äußeren Charakter. Im Inneren galt es, Trittschalldämmungen in den Gängen und Schall hemmende Leichtbauzwischenwände einzubauen, ohne die fließenden Räume mit ihren zeittypischen Farben zu beeinträchtigen. Außerdem waren Treppengeländer zu erhöhen und Beläge zu erneuern. Gewisse Bauteile wie Fenstergriffe und einige Faserzementprodukte sind noch heute im Handel. Anderes musste unauffällig durch Neues ersetzt werden. Trotz bautechnisch einschneidender Maßnahmen, etwa im Bereich des Brandschutzes, hat das Bauwerk Flair und Lockerheit der Aufbruchzeit nach der Wiederaufbauphase bewahrt. Davon zeugen nicht zuletzt da und dort einige typische frühe Kunststoffbauteile.

The building's location and structuring within the urban development ar!ea above the Dornbirner Ach River is characterized by stupendous elegance. It was built as the Federal Textile Engineering School in 1958 by German Meusburger and Willi Ramersdorfer. The volume of the aularian hall begins jauntily at the edge of the street. Next to it begins a slender and tall one-hip wing of classrooms that is answered with a lower and wider, double-layered second wing of classrooms. A connecting entrance hall that also leads to the former workshop in the back opens towards the garden court facing the river. The small new building on stilts over the underground garage to the south east is casually integrated within the overall structure. However, the fifties were a fast-living time in terms of structural physics and construction details. Therefore, the school was left vacant and considered a ruin when it was closed in 1981. Finally, the city and province were persuaded by committed architects and urban planners to not tear down the main building, but renovate it to serve the new school. Such landmark preservation demands for a building of this period are rare. The windows were replaced with new elements only slighter wider in profile despite their insulation that were designed by the architects. On the inside, it was important to use sound-impact insulation in the halls and and sound damping separating paneling without detracting from the colors, which are typical for buildings from that time. Banisters had to be raised and floors had to be renovated as well. Some components such as window handles and some fibre cement products are still available in stores today. Other things had to replaced with inconspicuous new parts. Despite significant structural changes in the field of fire protection, for example, the building has the flair and sense of ease that marked the beginning of the economic recovery after the war. Early synthetic elements that are typical of the time placed here and there underline this impression.

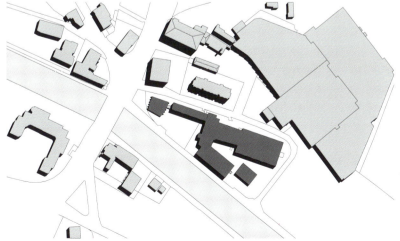

1999
Dornbirn, Austria
Bauherrschaft | Client: Stadt Dornbirn, Land Vorarlberg
Statik | Structural engineering: Mader & Flatz
Ziviltechniker GmbH, Bregenz
Mitarbeit | Assistence: Nives Pavkovic
Publikation | Publication: Architektur Aktuell 234/244,
Juli/August 2000; Architektur & Bauforum, 210, 1 – 2/2001;
baumeister, B10, 2001

192 Erneuerungen Refurbishments

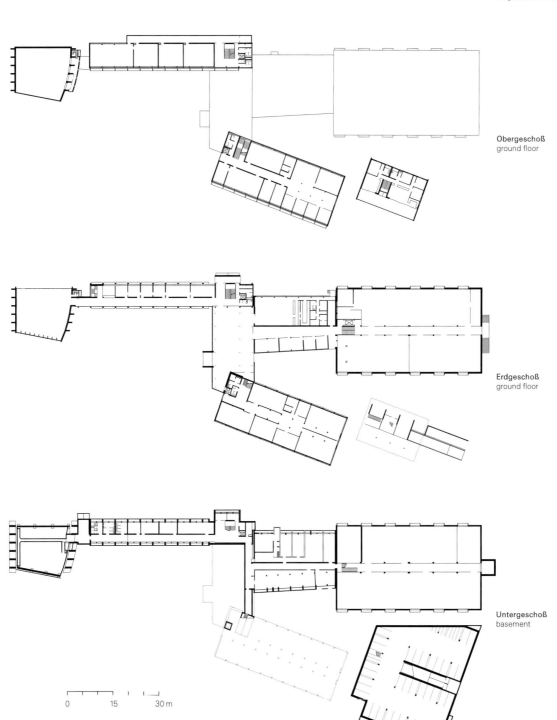

Längsschnitt
longitudinal section

Obergeschoß
ground floor

Erdgeschoß
ground floor

Untergeschoß
basement

0   15   30 m

Konstruktiv galt es unter anderem, die architektonisch eindrucksvollen Fassaden der ehemaligen Wirkerei mit ihren bauphyikalisch abenteuerlichen, herausstehenden Fensterkästen wärmetechnisch zufrieden stellend zu sanieren. Als Quellen wurden Wochenschaufilme der Eröffnung beigezogen, aus denen hervorging, dass die Fenster zu Beginn aus Holz und außenbündig angeschlagen waren. Offenbar wurden jedoch bald weiter innen Metallfenster eingesetzt. Statt wie mit bisher nur drei Zentimetern Heraklith wurde eine Außendämmung von acht Zentimetern Stärke an den Betonkrägen aufgebracht. Zusammen mit einer Fensterkonstruktion auf verdeckten Rahmen gelang es, die flachen Erkerräume an dem neu als Bibliothek und Ausstellungshalle genutzten Gebäude wieder herzustellen und die Innenräume der ursprünglichen Intention gemäß wirken zu lassen. Die etwas stärkeren Dimensionen und daher leicht veränderten Proportionen der Rahmenstirnen wurden in Kauf genommen. Raumakustische Maßnahmen sind so gesetzt, dass die Betonrippendecke erkennbar bleibt

In terms of construction, the objective was to refurbish the architecturally impressive façade of the former workshop in a manner that would satisfy the need for an adequate insulation solution for the structurally daring, protruding window elements. Old newsreels of the inauguration were viewed to establish that the timber windows had initially featured hinges on the outside. However, it seems that these were soon replaced with metal windows mounted on the inside. An eight-centimeter layer of Heraklith insulation then replaced the three-centimeter of insulation used earlier on the cement window collars. It was possible to create a concealed window frame structure and also to recreate the flat oriel rooms that serve as the library and exhibition hall in the newly refurbished building without changing the original architectural intention and effect of these rooms. The somewhat larger dimensions and the slightly altered proportions of the narrow sides of the frame were accepted as part of the new solution. The acoustic damping measures that were employed were designed to allow the cement-rib to remain recognizable.

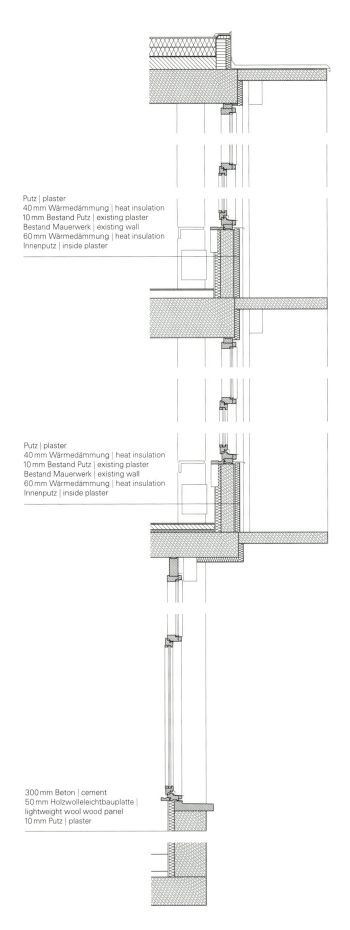

Putz | plaster
40 mm Wärmedämmung | heat insulation
10 mm Bestand Putz | existing plaster
Bestand Mauerwerk | existing wall
60 mm Wärmedämmung | heat insulation
Innenputz | inside plaster

Putz | plaster
40 mm Wärmedämmung | heat insulation
10 mm Bestand Putz | existing plaster
Bestand Mauerwerk | existing wall
60 mm Wärmedämmung | heat insulation
Innenputz | inside plaster

300 mm Beton | cement
50 mm Holzwolleleichtbauplatte | lightweight wool wood panel
10 mm Putz | plaster

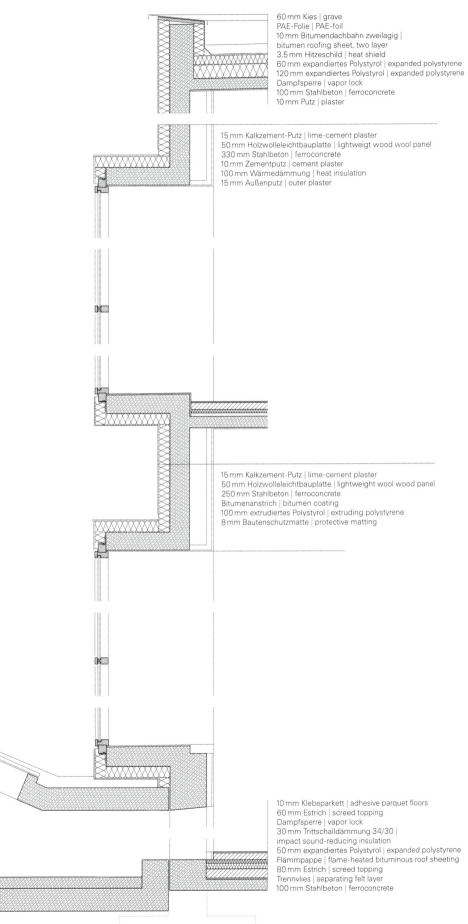

60 mm Kies | grave
PAE-Folie | PAE-foil
10 mm Bitumendachbahn zweilagig | bitumen roofing sheet, two layer
3,5 mm Hitzeschild | heat shield
60 mm expandiertes Polystyrol | expanded polystyrene
120 mm expandiertes Polystyrol | expanded polystyrene
Dampfsperre | vapor lock
100 mm Stahlbeton | ferroconcrete
10 mm Putz | plaster

15 mm Kalkzement-Putz | lime-cement plaster
50 mm Holzwolleleichtbauplatte | lightweigt wood wool panel
330 mm Stahlbeton | ferroconcrete
10 mm Zementputz | cement plaster
100 mm Wärmedämmung | heat insulation
15 mm Außenputz | outer plaster

15 mm Kalkzement-Putz | lime-cement plaster
50 mm Holzwolleleichtbauplatte | lightweight wool wood panel
250 mm Stahlbeton | ferroconcrete
Bitumenanstrich | bitumen coating
100 mm extrudiertes Polystyrol | extruding polystyrene
8 mm Bautenschutzmatte | protective matting

10 mm Klebeparkett | adhesive parquet floors
60 mm Estrich | screed topping
Dampfsperre | vapor lock
30 mm Trittschalldämmung 34/30 | impact sound-reducing insulation
50 mm expandiertes Polystyrol | expanded polystyrene
Flämmpappe | flame-heated bituminous roof sheeting
80 mm Estrich | screed topping
Trennvlies | separating felt layer
100 mm Stahlbeton | ferroconcrete

Christian Lenz

Motorschiff Vorarlberg, Neuer Innenausbau
Motorschiff Vorarlberg, Interior Renovation

Der erneuernden Innengestaltung des Bodenseeschiffs MS Vorarlberg lag ein Bestand vor, der – bei Schiffen selbstverständlich – von der Stromlinienform diktiert wurde. Viele Linien im Grundriss waren gebogen, es gab kein rechtwinkliges Ordnungsprinzip, wie es bei Häusern meistens der Fall ist. Die auf Schiffen übliche hohe Personendichte, geringe Raumhöhen und eine aufs Notwendige minimierte Stahlkonstruktion waren weiters zu berücksichtigen. Für die neuen Böden kam das im Schiffbau verbreitete Doussier-Holz zur Anwendung. Ein Hochzug mit Kehle entlang den Wänden aus dem gleichen Holz ist nicht bloß reinigungsfreundlich, sondern folgt dem Prinzip gerundeter Raumkanten, das ebenso beim Übergang von der Wand zur Decke gilt. Der Raum gewinnt damit einen dynamischen Charakter, wie es vielen Verkehrsmitteln entspricht. Der geringen Raumhöhe begegnet die Gestaltung mit einer weißen, die Sonnenkringel des Wellenspiels reflektierenden Hochglanzbeschichtung an der Decke, deren Wirkung den Plafond um die Höhe der helleren und daher gespiegelten Fenster virtuell anhebt und räumlichen Druck wegnimmt. Mit einem den Schall dämpfenden Deckenfeld aus Buchenleisten wird außerdem der Kernbereich des Hauptdecks, wo beim Einschiffen am meisten Unruhe entsteht, in raumakustischer Hinsicht verbessert. Die Tische und Sessel der Speisesäle wurden mehrheitlich aus der Vielfalt zeitgenössischer Serienproduktionen ausgewählt. Spezielle Nutzungsansprüche erforderten jedoch den Einbau umlaufender, gepolsterter Wandbänke wie beispielsweise in der Bar auf dem Sonnendeck. Zu den der Bequemlichkeit der Fahrgäste dienenden Maßnahmen kontrastiert die knappe Gestaltung der Treppen, wo es um Funktionalität auf beengtem Raum geht und um jene auf Schiffen zwingende Reduktion auf das Notwendige, die sich vom begrenzten Raum auf die Gestaltung überträgt und Funktionsabläufe sowie Details erfasst, sodass jene spezifische Übereinstimmung von Form und Ausdruck entstehen konnte, die den Schiffbau seit Jahrhunderten prägt und viele Architekten im frühen 20. Jahrhundert nachhaltig beeindruckte.

The renovation of the interiors of the MS Vorarlberg Lake Constance steamer was dictated by the streamlined shape of the ship. Many of the lines in the floor plan were bent, there was no right-angle sense of order, as is generally the case with houses. The high density of passengers common to a ship, the low ceilings and steel construction reduced to its bare minimum also had to be taken into account. Doussier planking, which is usually used in ship building, was used for the ships' floors. High grooved stays along the walls made of the same timber can be easily cleaned and complement the rounded edges of the rooms. It also serves as a transition from the wall to the roof. This adds to the dynamics of the room, in keeping with the practices in of many modes of transportation. The lowness of the ceilings is countered with a white, high-gloss roof finish that reflects the interplay of sun rays on the waves of the lake. This virtually raises the ceiling to the level of the light and therefore also reflects the windows, minimizing the sense of pressure on the room. The central area of the main deck was reinforced with birch timber slats to improve acoustic damping in this area of the craft, which is the most frequented area during embarkation. The tables and chairs in the dining rooms were mainly chosen from the ample selection of available mass produced furniture. Special functional requirements made it necessary to fit continuous cushioned benches surrounding the bar and along the sun deck. The reduced design of the stairs contrasts with amenities intended for the passengers. This functionality in an extremely tight space and the reduction to what is essential that is imperative on a ship made it necessary to integrate both functional processes and details in the design. Thus there is a convergence of form and expression here that has defined shipbuilding for centuries and which left a lasting impression on architects at the beginning of the 20th century.

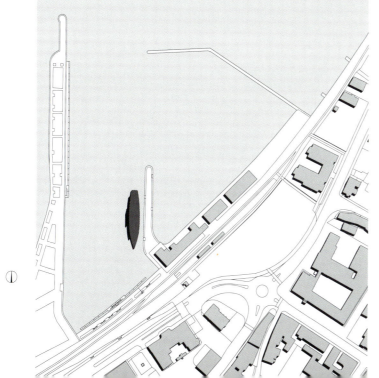

2000
Bregenz, Austria
Bauherrschaft | Client: ÖBB Bodenseeschifffahrt, Bregenz
Mitarbeit | Assistence: Helmut Brunner
Publikation | Publication: Der Standard, 04.07.2000

198 Erneuerungen Refurbishments

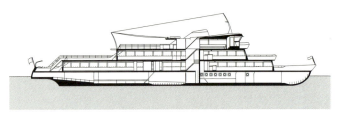

0 10 20 m

Längsschnitt
longitudinal section

Querschnitt
cross section

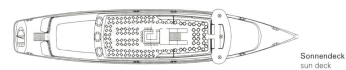

Sonnendeck
sun deck

Zwischendeck
between deck

Hauptdeck
main deck

22 mm Doussier geölt massiv | solid Doussier wood, oiled
9 mm Birkensperrholz | birch chipboard
Ausgleichsspachtelung | evening primer layer
Stahlblech Bestand | existing sheet metal
Stahlkonstruktion dazwischen Dämmung |
steel construction with insulation in between
Dampfsperre | vapor lock
Hohlraum | hollow space
beschichtete Sperrholzplatte |
coated chipboard panel

Stahlblech Bestand | existing sheet metal
Stahlkonstruktion dazwischen Dämmung |
steel construction with insulation in between
Dampfsperre | vapor lock
Hohlraum/Lüftung/Radiatoren |
hollow space/ventilation/radiators
Akustikmatte | acoustic mat
furnierte Sperrholzplatte Doussier gewachst |
waxed Doussier vener chipboard panel

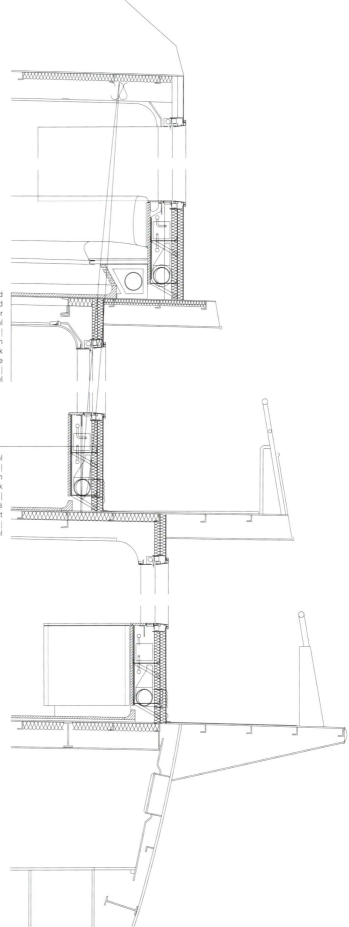

Weitere Werke auszugsweise
Catalogue of Projects

Auszeichnungen
Awards

MitarbeiterInnen
Collaborators

Biographien
Biographies

Hermann Kaufmann und Christian Lenz

1984 | Haus Rüscher
Schnepfau
Bauherr | Client: Maria und Heinz Rüscher

1994 | Werkhalle Übelhör
Höchst
Bauherr | Client: Eugen Übelhör

1994 | Küchenhaus Allgäuer
Klaus
Bauherr | Client: Wolfgang Allgäuer
Publikation | Publication: Ottagono, 3/1988; Holzbaukunst in Vorarlberg, Eugen-Ruß-Verlag 1990; Schweizer Holzzeitung, H42, 10/1990; Zeitgemäßes Gestalten und Konstruieren mit Holz, 1.Auflg 5/1991

1995 | Umbau Christensen
Dornbirn
Bauherr | Client: Heide und John Christensen

1987 | Gemeindesaal |1
Klaus
Bauherr | Client: Gemeinde Klaus
Publikation | Publication: architektur aktuell, 23.Jg., 125/1988; Ottagono, 3/1988; Ländlicher Raum, 1/1989; Schweizer Holzzeitung, H42, 10/1990; Baukunst in Vorarlberg seit 1980

1989 | Gemeindesaal
Hittisau
Bauherr | Client: Gemeinde Hittisau
Publikation | Publication: Ländlicher Raum,1/1989; architektur & wirtschaft, Journal internat. Bodenseeregion, 1993; Architektur Beispiele Eternit, Dietmar Steiner, 1994; Schweizer Holzzeitung, H42, 10/1990; Baukunst in Vorarlberg seit 1980

1993 | Büro- und Betriebserweiterung |2
Rieger-Orgelbau
Schwarzach
Bauherr | Client: Firma Rieger
Publikation | Publication: baumeister, 5/1996; architektur & wirtschaft, Journal internat. Bodenseeregion, 1993; Neue Architektur in Vorarlberg, Bauten der neunziger Jahre, 1997; Architektur für die Arbeitswelt, Birkhäuser, 1995; Baukunst in Vorarlberg seit 1980

1995 | Turn- und Festsaal |3
Muntlix
Bauherr | Client: Gemeinde Zwischenwasser
Publikation | Publication: baumeister, 1/1996; Neue Architektur in Vorarlberg, Bauten der neunziger Jahre, 1997; Baukunst in Vorarlberg seit 1980

1996 | Raiffeisenbank
Schwarzach
Bauherr | Client: Raiffeisenbank

2001 | Sanierung Diözesanhaus
Feldkirch
Bauherr | Client: Diözese Feldkirch
Publikation | Publication: Baukunst in Vorarlberg seit 1980

2001 | Naturschau Rüschareal
Dornbirn
Bauherr | Client: FM Hämmerle Bauträger GesmbH, Stadt Dornbirn

2001 | Pfarrsaal
Höchst
Bauherr | Client: Pfarrgemeinde Höchst

Hermann Kaufmann

1984 | Haus Gasser
Schnepfau
Bauherr | Client: Rosmarie und Karlheinz Gasser

1984 | Umbau Greber/Lang
Dornbirn
Bauherr | Client: Katharina und Alois Lang, Maria und Gebhard Greber

1985 | Haus Meusburger
Bizau
Bauherr | Client: Josefine und Herbert Meusburger

1985 | Doppelhaus Tomas
Egg
Bauherr | Client: Resi und Werner Tomas, Maria und Reinhard Tomas
Publikation | Publication: VN-Beilage, 1.Vlbg. Bauherrenpreis, Die Kunst normal zu bauen

1985 | Halle Ost Kaufmann Holz-AG |4
Reuthe
Bauherr | Client: Kaufmann Holz AG
Publikation | Publication: Holzkurier, 44. Jg., 6/1989

1987 | Haus Schwarzmann
Alberschwende
Bauherr | Client: Angelika und Erich Schwarzmann

1987 | Haus Voppichler
Egg
Bauherr | Client: Ewald Voppichler

1985 – 1987 | Haus Kaufmann
Mellau
Bauherr | Client: Gerhard Kaufmann
Publikation | Publication: Holzbauten in Vorarlberg, Rheticus-Gesellschaft, 1995

1986 – 1987 | Haus Rüscher
Schnepfau
Bauherr | Client: Diana und Anton Rüscher

1988 | Haus Kaufmann
Reuthe
Bauherr | Client: Anna und Ernst Kaufmann
Publikation | Publication: schweizer holzzeitung, H. 42, 10/1990; Zuhause Wohnen, 11/1992

1988 | Kapelle Reuthe
Vorsäß
Bauherr | Client: Genossenschaft Schnellvorsäß

1988 | Haus Riedmann
Rankweil
Bauherr | Client: Karin und Michael Riedmann

1989 | Technischer Dienst Kaufmann Holz-AG
Reuthe
Bauherr | Client: Kaufmann Holz AG

1989 | Haus Jäger
Bezau
Bauherr | Client: Irmgard und Fritz Jäger
Publikation | Publication: VN-Beilage, 2.Vlbg. Bauherrenpreis, Die Kunst normal zu bauen

1989 | Adeg
Nenzing
Bauherr | Client: ADEG Österreich Handels AG, Lauterach

1989 | Wartehäuschen Wälderbus
Bregenzerwald versch. Standorte
Bauherr | Client: Regionalplanungsgemeinschaft Bregenzerwald

1989 | Haus Heim
Dornbirn
Bauherr | Client: Christine und Herbert Heim

1990 | Gemeinschaftsgebäude und |5
Feuerwehr Bizau
Bauherr | Client: Gemeinde Bizau

1990 | Solarschule
Dafins
Bauherr | Client: Gemeinde Zwischenwasser
Entwurf | Design: mit Walter Unterrainer
Publikation | Publication: Holz Bulletin, H.33/1993

1990 | Abbundhalle Kaufmann |6
Reuthe
Bauherr | Client: Zimmerei Michael Kaufmann
Publikation | Publication: Holz Bulletin, H.27/1991; BauArt3, Zschokke Walter, Wien 1992; Neue Häuser, Architektur Fotografien Margherita Spiluttini, 1993; Architektur Beispiele Eternit, Dietmar Steiner, 1994; Architecture + Detail, Bauen mit Faserzement, H.4/1995; Architektur für die Arbeitswelt, Birkhäuser, 1995; Gestalten mit der Welle, K. Krämer Verlag, 1998; Architektur & Wohnen, Heft 3/01; pro:Holz zuschnitt 1/2001

1990 | Doppelhaus Kaufmann/Büchele
Wolfurt
Bauherr | Client: Irmgard und Michael Büchele, Ursula und Hermann Kaufmann

1990 | Lagerhalle und Büro Kaufmann Holz-AG
Wolfurt
Bauherr | Client: Kaufmann Holz AG, Reuthe

1990 | Umbau Steurer
Bezau
Bauherr | Client: Gerhard Steurer

1990 | Umbau „Sammerhaus"
Wolfurt
Bauherr | Client: Helmut Böhler

1990 | Umbau Otten
Hohenems
Bauherr | Client: Eva Feuerstein, Bregenz

1990 | Umbau Stadel Kloster Mehrerau
Bregenz
Bauherr | Client: Kloster Mehrerau

1991 | Umbau Rüscher
Andelsbuch
Bauherr | Client: Ingrid und Rudolf Rüscher

1991 | Pfarrhof Bildstein
Bildstein
Bauherr | Client: Pfarre Maria Bildstein

 |1
 |2
 |3
 |4
 |5
 |6

Weitere Werke auzugsweise — Catalogue of Projects

1991 | Haus Fürst
Dornbirn
Bauherr | Client: Aloisia Fürst

1991 | Adeg
Lustenau
Bauherr | Client: ADEG Österreich Handels AG, Lauterach

1991 | Abbundhalle Sohm
Alberschwende
Bauherr | Client: Zimmerei Sohm

1992 | Volta
Lauterach
Bauherr | Client: Hinteregger Bau GmbH, Bregenz
Publikation | Publication: schweizer holzzeitung, 20/1994

1992 | Abbundhalle Kaufmann Holz-AG |7
Reuthe
Bauherr | Client: Kaufmann Holz AG, Wolfurt
Publikation | Publication: baumeister, 10/1996; architektur & wirtschaft, Journal internat. Bodenseeregion, 1993; Neue Architektur in Vorarlberg, Bauten der neunziger Jahre, 1997; Architektur für die Arbeitswelt, Birkhäuser, 1995

1993 | Umbau Bischof
Bezau
Bauherr | Client: Evi und Peter Bischof

1993 | Strickwarenproduktionshalle Bischof
Reuthe
Bauherr | Client: Peter Bischof, Bezau
Publikation | Publication: Holz Bulletin, H40/1995; Architektur für die Arbeitswelt, Birkhäuser, 1995

1993 | Tischlerei Böhler
Wolfurt
Bauherr | Client: Tischlerei Böhler

1993 | Umbau Meusburger
Wolfurt
Bauherr | Client: Hans Meusburger

1993 | Haus Berchtold
Ludmannsdorf
Bauherr | Client: Martina und Andreas Berchtold
Publikation | Publication: Architekturjournal Wettbewerbe, H157, 158, 1, 2/1997; Architektur & Bauforum, Standardhäuser, Die Häuslbauer, AZW, 1997

1993 | Haus Breuss
Weiler
Bauherr | Client: Cornelia Breuss

1993 | Zimmerei Berchtold
Bezau
Bauherr | Client: Wilfried Berchtold

1993 | Bären
Mellau
Bauherr | Client: Bad Reuthe Frick GesmbH, Reuthe

1993 | Clubheim FC Bizau
Bizau
Bauherr | Client: Gemeinde Bizau

1993 | Haus Hinteregger
Kennelbach-Kusterberg
Bauherr | Client: Hinteregger G. Hoch- und Tiefbau GesmbH, Bregenz

1991 – 1993 | Doppelhaus Sperger/Waibel
Lustenau
Bauherr | Client: Monika und Heinz Sperger
Entwurf | Design: mit Walter Unterrainer
Publikation | Publication: deutsche bauzeitung, Jg. 128, 8/1994

1994 | Haus Schmiedinger
Schwarzenberg
Bauherr | Client: Sonja und Wolfgang Schmiedinger

1994 | Umbau Altes Schulhaus
Bildstein
Bauherr | Client: Gemeinde Bildstein

1994 | Haus Bösch
Lustenau
Bauherr | Client: Brigitte und Bernd Bösch
Publikation | Publication: Neue Architektur in Vorarlberg, Bauten der neunziger Jahre, 1997; Holzvariationen, Verlag f. Bauwesen Berlin, 1998

1994 | Produktionshalle Glas Marte |8
Bregenz
Bauherr | Client: Glas Marte GesmbH & Co KG

1994 | Clubgebäude FC Egg
Egg
Bauherr | Client: FC Egg

1994 | Haus Galehr
Dornbirn
Bauherr | Client: Ulrike und Josef Galehr

1994 | Adeg Eberle
Hittisau
Bauherr | Client: Reinhold Eberle und Mitgesellschafter GesmbR

1995 | Verbauung Häldele
Bizau
Bauherr | Client: Gemeinde Bizau

1995 | Aufstockung Bürogebäude Glas Marte
Bregenz
Bauherr | Client: Glas Marte GesmbH & Co KG

1995 | Haus Fischer
Lech
Bauherr | Client: Claudia und Bernd Fischer

1995 | Friedhofskapelle Bizau |9
Bizau
Bauherr | Client: Gemeinde Bizau
Publikation | Publication: Beton Zement, Technik und Architektur, 02/1996

1996 | Doppelhaus Schiestl/Nosko
Dornbirn
Bauherr | Client: Margit Nosko und Gunter Max Schiestl

1996 | Zubau Haus Sausgruber
Höchst
Bauherr | Client: Ilga und Herbert Sausgruber

1996 | Haus Sutterlüty
Egg
Bauherr | Client: Kathrin und Jürgen Sutterlüty

1996 | Umbau Stärk
Dornbirn
Bauherr | Client: Ursula und Wilhelm Stärk

1996 | Zubau Hotel Widderstein
Schröcken
Bauherr | Client: G. Hinteregger Bau GmbH., Bregenz

1996 | Umbau Raiffeisenbank |10
Schwarzenberg
Bauherr | Client: Raiffeisenbank Mittelbregenzerwald, Egg

1996 | Polytechnische Schule
Hittisau
Bauherr | Client: Schulerhalterverband

1996 | Haus Vögel
Sulberg-Thal
Bauherr | Client: Karin und Walter Vögel

1997 | Clubgebäude FC Bizau
Bizau
Bauherr | Client: FC Bizau

1997 | Umbau Haus Wirth
Andelsbuch
Bauherr | Client: Rosi und Anton Wirth

1997 | Umbau Haus Feldkircher
Egg
Bauherr | Client: Josef Feldkircher

1997 | Umbau Haus Rupp
Fußach
Bauherr | Client: Arno Rupp

1997 | Haus Natter
Mellau
Bauherr | Client: Annette und Othmar Natter
Publikation | Publication: Trend Spezial 1/97

1997 | Stationen Sonnenkopf Bergbahnen |11
Klösterle
Bauherr | Client: Klostertaler Bergbahnen GmbH, Innsbruck
Publikation | Publication: Architektur und Seilbahnen, Architektur Forum Tirol, 3/2000

1998 | Sporthalle
Klösterle
Bauherr | Client: Gemeinde Klösterle

1998 | Reihenhausanlage
Alberschwende
Bauherr | Client: Kohler Wohnbau, Andelsbuch

1998 | Haus Burger
Wolfurt
Bauherr | Client: Eveline und Jürgen Burger
Publikation | Publication: Die Presse, 17.2.99; Der Zimmermeister, 2/99; Holzbau, Österr. Wirtschaftsverl., 1 – 2/99

1998 | Rheindeltahaus
Fußach
Bauherr | Client: Amt d. Vorarlberger Landesregierung, Bregenz
Publikation | Publication: Weisstanne, Broschüre d. Vorarlb. Landwirtschaftskammer, 1999; Naturschutzgebiet Rheindelta, 1998

1998 | Reihenhausanlage
Lingenau
Bauherr | Client: Kohler Wohnbau

1998 | Umbau Haus Ruepp
Dornbirn
Bauherr | Client: Carmen und Martin Ruepp

1998 | Umbau Raiffeisenbank
Andelsbuch
Bauherr | Client: Raiffeisenbank Mittelbregenzerwald, Egg

1999 | Umbau Raiffeisenbank
Bezau
Bauherr | Client: Raiffeisenbank Bezau, Bizau, Mellau
Publikation | Publication: Architekturforum Vorarlberg, Arch. + Wirtsch.Förder.Verlag, 1999

1999 | Wohnanlage Spielerstraße
Hohenems
Bauherr | Client: Hinteregger Bau und Projektentwicklung GmbH, Bregenz

1999 | Schule und Saal |12
Bizau
Bauherr | Client: Gemeinde Bizau

1999 | Umbau Haus Zündel
Egg
Bauherr | Client: Karlheinz Zündel

1999 | Haus Rohner/Dobler
Hard
Bauherr | Client: Hildegard Dobler und Felix Rohner

1999 | Stationen Wildgunten
Mellau
Bauherr | Client: Bergbahnen Mellau

1999 | Umbau Krone
Schwarzenberg
Bauherr | Client: Elfriede Kahl

1999 | Haus Ritter
Lustenau
Bauherr | Client: Gabi und Kurt Ritter

1999 | Wohnanlage
Egg
Bauherr | Client: Nägelebau GesmbH & Co, Sulz

1999 | Doppelhaus Natter/Kapfer
Lauterach
Bauherr | Client: Familie Natter und Kapfer

1999 | Büroerweiterung Pfanner
Lauterach
Bauherr | Client: Pfanner Getränke GesmbH

2000 | Reihenhausanlage
Egg
Bauherr | Client: Hiller Wohnbau und Immobilien GmbH, Bregenz

 |7

 |8

 |9

 |10

 |11

 |12

2000 | Biomasseheizwerk
Mellau
Bauherr | Client: Vorarlberger Kraftwerke AG, Bregenz

2000 | Physiotherapie Rüscher
Andelsbuch
Bauherr | Client: Martina und Michael Rüscher

2000 | Haus Kopf
Au
Bauherr | Client: Maria und Thomas Kopf

2000 | Kindergarten
Hohenems/Reute
Bauherr | Client: Stadt Hohenems

2000 | Produktionshalle Gmeiner
Wolfurt
Bauherr | Client: Fidel Gmeiner GesmbH & Co

2000 | „Dorfhus"
Krumbach
Bauherr | Client: Errichtergemeinschaft Dorfhus

2000 | Haus Dietrich
Lech
Bauherr | Client: Maria und Werner Dietrich

2000 | Sparmarkt
Mellau
Bauherr | Client: Spar Österr. Warenhandels-AG, Dornbirn

2000 | Bürozentrale Sutterlüty
Egg
Bauherr | Client: Sutterlüty GesmbH & Co

2000 | Clubheim FC Schwarzenberg
Schwarzenberg
Bauherr | Client: FC Schwarzenberg

2000 | Rettungsheim
Egg
Bauherr | Client: Gemeinde Egg
Publikation | Publication: 50 Jahre ÖRK Rettung Egg, Eröffnungsfestschrift Oktober 1999

2000 | Pfarrheim
Koblach
Bauherr | Client: Pfarrgemeinde Koblach

2000 | Greußinghof
Lauterach
Bauherr | Client: Ursula und Elmar Greußing

2000 | Bank für Tirol und Vorarlberg
Hohenems
Bauherr | Client: Bank für Tirol und Vorarlberg, Innsbruck

2000 | Haus Schäfer/Kleindienst
Feldkirch-Tisis
Bauherr | Client: Sieglinde und Kurt Kleindienst, Theresia und Albrecht Schäfer
Entwurf | Design: mit Walter Unterrainer

2000 | Flugdach Holzlagerhalle
Metzler H. KG
Bezau
Bauherr | Client: Metzler H. KG

2001 | Büroneubau Andorfer
Bregenz
Bauherr | Client: Stefan Andorfer

2001 | Forsthaus
Regentsweiler/D
Bauherr | Client: Fürstlich Hohenzollerische Hofkammer, Siegmaringen/D

2001 | Biomasseheizwerk
Gaschurn
Bauherr | Client: Vorarlberger Kraftwerke AG, Bregenz

2001 | Haus Kohler
Schwarzenberg
Bauherr | Client: Angelika und Sigfried Kohler

2001 | Umbau Gemeindehaus |13
Krumbach
Bauherr | Client: Gemeinde Krumbach

2001 | Erweiterung Dorner Electronic
Egg
Bauherr | Client: Dorner Electronic

2001 | Angelika-Kaufmann-Saal
Schwarzenberg
Bauherr | Client: Gemeinde Schwarzenberg

2001 | Bauhof Bildstein
Bildstein
Bauherr | Client: Gemeinde Bildstein

2001 | Sanierung Bauernhaus Häfele
Mellau
Bauherr | Client: Dorothea und Georg Häfele

2001 | Büro- und Betriebsgebäude Zimmerei Dobler
Röthis
Bauherr | Client: Dobler Bau GesmbH

2001 | Büroneubau „Die Drei"
Dornbirn
Bauherr | Client: Errichtergemeinschaft Bruno Welzenbach und Mitbesitzer

2002 | Kirche Kennelbach
Kennelbach
Bauherr | Client: Pfarre Kennelbach

2002 | Zubau Naturhotel Chesa Valisa
Hirschegg
Bauherr | Client: Sigi und Klaus Kessler

2002 | Haus Widerin
Wolfurt
Bauherr | Client: Karin und Martin Widerin

2002 | Umbau Pfarramt
Schnepfau
Bauherr | Client: Gemeinde Schnepfau Immobilienverwaltung GmbH & Co KEG

2002 | Gewerbepark Wälderhaus |14
Bezau
Bauherr | Client: Bau- und Brennstoffhandels-gesmbH & Co

2002 | Lebensmittelmarkt Sutterlüty
Weiler
Bauherr | Client: Sutterlüty GesmbH & Co, Egg

2002 | Erweiterung Bad Reuthe |15
Reuthe
Bauherr | Client: Bad Reuthe Frick GesmbH
Entwurf | Design: mit Walter Unterrainer

2002 | Bau- und Abfallwirtschaftsnetz
Lech
Bauherr | Client: Gemeinde Lech

2002 – 2004 | Bundesgymnasium
Bludenz
Bauherr | Client: Bundesimmobiliengesellschaft, Wien

Christian Lenz

1982 | Haus Winder
Schwarzach
Bauherr | Client: Bernadette und Gerhard Winder

1984 | Haus Köb
Wolfurt
Bauherr | Client: Siegfried Köb

1984 | Umbau Haus Kögler
Lustenau
Bauherr | Client: Susanne und Peter Kögler

1985/1988/1995/1998 | Zu- und Umbauten Zweiradfachgeschäft Loitz
Lauterach
Bauherr | Client: Reinhard Loitz

1985 | Haus Schelling
Schwarzach
Bauherr | Client: Peter Schelling

1987 | Umbau Schöllerbank
Bregenz
Bauherr | Client: SKWB Schöllerbank AG

1987 | Haus Sonnberger
Dornbirn
Bauherr | Client: Karlheinz Sonnberger

1987 – 1988 | Haus Bohle |16
Dornbirn-Kehlegg
Bauherr | Client: Barbara und Achim Bohle

1987 – 1989 | Umbau Haus Grabher
Lustenau
Bauherr | Client: Manfred Grabher

1988 – 1990 | Wohnanlage |17
Rauhholzsiedlung
Hard
Bauherr | Client: Hofsteig Wohnbau GmbH
Entwurf | Design: mit Helmut Dietrich
Publikation | Publication: Architektur in Vorarlberg seit 1960, Eugen Russ Verlag, 1993; Baukunst in Vorarlberg seit 1980, Verlag Hatje, 1998; Architektur Beispiele Eternit, Verlag Löcker, Wien, Dietmar Steiner

1989 – 1990 | Haus Kohler |18
Schwarzach
Bauherr | Client: Dagmar und Gebhard Kohler
Publikation | Publication: Architektur in Vorarlberg seit 1960, Eugen Russ Verlag; 1993

1989 – 1990 | Umbau Haus Bechtold |19
Schwarzach
Bauherr | Client: Ingrid Adamer und Ekkehard Bechtold
Publikation | Publication: Architektur in Vorarlberg seit 1960, Eugen Russ Verlag, 1993; Raum + Wohnen Nr. 6/91, Internationales Magazin für Architektur

1989 – 1990 | Haus Flatz
Schwarzach
Bauherr | Client: Andrea und Josef Flatz

1990 | Zu- und Umbau Haus Mathis
Dornbirn
Bauherr | Client: Klaus Mathis

1991 – 1993 | Sportclubgebäude |20
Schwarzach
Bauherr | Client: Gemeinde Schwarzach
Entwurf | Design: mit Helmut Dietrich
Publikation | Publication: Baukunst in Vorarlberg seit 1980, Verlag Hatje, 1998

1990 – 1992 | Haus Breier |21
Lochau
Bauherr | Client: Reingard und Christoph Breier

1990 – 1991 | Umbau Haus Herburger
Feldkirch
Bauherr | Client: Raphaela Stefandl und Ulrich Herburger

1991 – 1994 | Haus Rigger
Dornbirn
Bauherr | Client: Renate und Alfons Rigger

1991 – 1992 | Umbau Haus Engler
Rankweil
Bauherr | Client: Eduard Engler

1992 | Friedhof Watzenegg
Dornbirn
Bauherr | Client: Stadt Dornbirn
Entwurf | Design: mit Hans Zaugg

1992 | Sanierung Mehrfamilienhaus
Lauterach
Bauherr | Client: I&R Schertler/Flatz

1991 – 1992 | Umbau Wohnhaus/Zubau Atelier
Schwarzach
Bauherr | Client: Bernhard und Johannes Kaufmann

1988 – 1993 | Seilbahnstation Grießkareckbahn
Wagrein
Bauherr | Client: Bergbahnen AG Wagrein
Entwurf | Design: mit Helmut Dietrich
Publikation | Publication: Neue Häuser Architekturfotografie Margherita Spiluttini, Löcker Verlag, 1993; Architektur und Seilbahnen – von der Tradition zur Moderne – Architekturforum Tirol, 2000

1994 | Büroerweiterung I&R Schertler
Lauterach
Bauherr | Client: I&R Schertler
Entwurf | Design: mit Helmut Dietrich

1994 | Wohnanlage „Köb-Erlosen"
Dornbirn
Bauherr | Client: I&R Schertler
Entwurf | Design: mit Helmut Dietrich

|13

|14

|15

|16

|17

|18

205 Weitere Werke auszugsweise · Catalogue of Projects

1994 | Haus Kapp
Wolfurt
Bauherr | Client: Gerlinde und Norbert Kapp

1994 – 1995 | Umbau Haus Fulterer
Lustenau
Bauherr | Client: Manfred Fulterer

1994 – 1998 | Lagerhalle und Versand Firma Lenz
Schwarzach
Bauherr | Client: Andrea Lenz
Publikation | Publication: Baukunst in Vorarlberg seit 1980, Verlag Hatje, 1998

1995 | Haus Leu |22
Lauterach
Bauherr | Client: Eveline und Walter Leu
Publikation | Publication: Baukunst in Vorarlberg seit 1980, Verlag Hatje, 1998

1995 – 1996 | Umbau Mehrfamilienhaus Bahnhofstraße 1
Schwarzach
Bauherr | Client: Revital Bauträger GmbH

1995 – 1996 | Wohnanlage Bahnhofstraße 2
Schwarzach
Bauherr | Client: Revital Bauträger GmbH

1996 | Zu- und Umbau Haus Wilfried Breuss
Schwarzach
Bauherr | Client: Wilfried Breuss

1996 – 1997 | Haus Feichtinger |23
Hohenems
Bauherr | Client: Susanne und Arnold Feichtinger

1995 – 1998 | Umbau Haus Fink
Schwarzach
Bauherr | Client: Ruth und Walter Fink

1997 – 1998 | Erweiterung und |24
Aufstockung Fein-Elast Umwindewerk
Lustenau
Bauherr | Client: Fein-Elast Umwindewerk GmbH

1997 | Umbau Galerie c.art Prantl & Boch
Dornbirn
Bauherr | Client: Prantl & Boch GmbH

1996 | Wohnanlage Badgasse
Dornbirn
Bauherr | Client: Revital Bauträger GmbH

1997 | Haus Fitz
Gaschurn
Bauherr | Client: Manuela und Harald Fitz

1998 | Haus Brunner
Schwarzach
Bauherr | Client: Julia und Thomas Brunner

1999 | Sanierung Nächtigungshaus 2 Jugend- und Bildungshaus St. Arbogast
Bauherr | Client: Diözese/Jugend- und Bildungshaus St. Arbogast

2000 | Umbau Metzgerei Klopfer
Lauterach
Bauherr | Client: Christoph Klopfer

2001 | Sanierung Bürohaus Fulterer GesmbH
Lustenau
Bauherr | Client: Fulterer GesmbH

2001 | Umbau Haus Boch
Dornbirn
Bauherr | Client: Belinda und Hannes Boch

2001 | Umbau Restaurant Guth
Lauterach
Bauherr | Client: Thomas Guth

2001 | Wohnanlage Rickenbach
Wolfurt
Bauherr | Client: Revital Bauträger Gmbh

2002 | Haus Fulterer
Lustenau
Bauherr | Client: Vera Fulterer

2002 | Haus Sohm
Alberschwende
Bauherr | Client: Thomas Sohm

Auszeichnungen | Awards
Hermann Kaufmann

1996 | European Glulam Award
Ausstellungshalle, Murau

1997 | Vorarlberger Holzbaupreis
Wohnanlage Ölzbündt, Dornbirn
Wohnanlage Häldele, Bizau
Haus Arnold Schmid, Frastanz
Haus Othmar Natter, Mellau

1998 | Vorarlberger Holzbaupreis
Holzlagerhallen Metzler H. KG, Bezau
Lagerhalle Kaufmann Holz AG, Reuthe
Turn- und Festsaal, Muntlix

Vorarlberger Bauherrenpreis
Wohnanlage Ölzbündt, Dornbirn
Reithalle Probstei St. Gerold, St. Gerold

Markierung
Architekturforum Obersee, CH
Möbelfabrik Linth, Kaltbrunn, CH

1999 | Arge Alp Umweltpreis
Wohnanlage Ölzbündt, Dornbirn

Bauen in den Alpen
Reithalle Probstei St. Gerold, St. Gerold

European Glulam Award
Umbau Gymnasium Kloster Mehrerau, Bregenz

Röfix Althaussanierung
Fachhochschule (Alte Textilschule), Dornbirn

Haus der Zukunft
Preis für nachhaltiges Wirtschaften
Wohnanlage Ölzbündt, Dornbirn
Architekturbüro, Schwarzach
Haus Jürgen Burger, Wolfurt

Vorarlberger Holzbaupreis
Haus Beck-Faigle, Hard
Haus Anton Kaufmann, Reuthe
Fahrradbrücke, Gaißau
Rheindeltahaus, Fußach
Haus Rohner-Dobler, Hard

Vorarlberger Bauherrenpreis
Wohnanlage Neudorfstraße, Wolfurt
Impulszentrum Bregenzerwald, Egg
Biomasseheizwerk, Lech
Fachhochschule (Alte Textilschule), Dornbirn
Schule und Saal, Bizau

2001 | Vorarlberger Holzbaupreis
Haus Thomas Kopf, Au
Wohnanlage Neudorfstraße, Wolfurt
Haus Geissler, Wolfurt
Bauernhof Greussing, Lauterach

Auszeichnungen | Awards
Christian Lenz

1989 | European Glulam Award
Gemeindesaal, Klaus

1991 | Vorarlberger Bauherrenpreis
Rauhholzsiedlung, Hard

1997 | Vorarlberger Holzbaupreis
Doppelhaus Klosterwiesweg, Schwarzach

1998 | Vorarlberger Holzbaupreis
Turn- und Festsaal, Muntlix

1999 | European Glulam Award
Umbau Gymnasium Kloster Mehrerau, Bregenz

2000 | Haus der Zukunft
Preis für nachhaltiges Wirtschaften
Architekturbüro, Schwarzach

Staatspreis für Tourismus und Architektur
Aparentmenthaus Lechblick, Warth

Bauherrenpreis der Zentralvereinigung der Architekten Österreichs
Fachhochschule (Alte Textilschule), Dornbirn

2001 | Vorarlberger Holzbaupreis
Aparentmenthaus Lechblick, Warth

Vorarlberger Bauherrenpreis
Fachhochschule (Alte Textilschule), Dornbirn
Aparentmenthaus Lechblick, Warth

|19 |20 |21 |22 |23 |24

Hermann Kaufmann

MitarbeiterInnen:
Baumgartl Benjamin
Broger Ralph
Dünser Christoph
Fetz Doris
Hafner Carmen
Hammer Petra
Hämmerle Gerold
Hiebeler Stefan
Hockauf Gabriele
Junker Hartmut
Kalb Christoph
Kaufmann Norbert
Längle Martin
Martin Claudia
Roos Simone
Rümmele Martin
Seidler Harald
Wehinger Roland
Wiljotti Juliane

Ehemalige MitarbeiterInnen:
Amann Thomas
Bilgeri Wolfgang
Elmenreich Wolfgang
Ennulat Rolf
Erber Cord
Feuerstein Beate
Forer Richard
Gasser Silvia
Geutze Thomas
Gisinger Gerhard
Hafner Peter
Hagspiel Jürgen
Hammerer Wolfgang
Kargl Franz
Kaufmann Johannes
Kaufmann Ursula
Knünz Felix
Lamprecht Angela
Lanz Markus
Leuprecht Gerold
Meusburger Simone
Muxel Reinhard
Natter Gottfrieda
Neyer Herwig
Nußbaumer Daniela
Nußbaumer Peter
Pavkovic Nives
Ratz Alois
Rüf Albert
Rüscher Markus
Schneider Claudia
Steurer Elke
Steurer Susanne
Weratschnig Andreas
Wörndle Emil

FerialpraktikantInnen:
Benzer Walter
Böhler Birgit
Felder Michael
Feurstein Karin
Geser Alois
Hagen Ulrich
Kappaurer Miriam
Kazil Alex
Lampert Ralf
Larsen Sven
Mennel Thomas
Metzler Simon
Miatto Benjamin
Rhomberg Meinhard
Rüscher Markus
Schedler Robert
Spiegel Bernd
Wässer Lukas

Christian Lenz

MitarbeiterInnen:
Berktold Philipp
Brunner Helmut
Felder Sabine
Hafner Carmen
Hammer Petra
Matt Gerhard
Redlich Carsten

Ehemalige MitarbeiterInnen:
Bösch Gernot
Capello Francesco
Dittrich Wolfgang
Dünser Susanne
Erath Jürgen
Gmeiner Elmar
Hafner Jürgen
Huber Dietmar
Lamprecht Angela
Lohmann Edda
Mages Rudolf
Mathis Herbert
Meusburger Simone
Puchmayr Adolf
Rüdisser Elisabeth
Schedler Werner
Sommer Rudolf
Spiegel Bernd
Steurer Elke
Stickl Andreas

FerialpraktikantInnen:
Böhler Anna
Geser Alois
Giselbrecht Markus
Hampl Andreas
Kaufmann Philipp
Kazil Alexander
Larsen Sven
Mennel Thomas
Mohr Andreas

Hermann Kaufmann

wurde 1955 in Reuthe, Bregenzerwald geboren und wuchs auf in einer alten Zimmermannsfamilie. Den vom Großvater auf den Vater vererbten Betrieb führt heute sein Bruder Michael. Nach der Matura am Bundesgymnasium Bregenz folgte das Architekturstudium an der Technischen Hochschule Innsbruck und an der Technischen Universität Wien. Praktika bei Architekt Leopold Kaufmann und Architekt Prof. Ernst Hiesmayr ergänzten die Ausbildung. 1983 Gründung des eigenen Architekturbüros in Bürogemeinschaft mit Christian Lenz in Schwarzach. Lehrtätigkeit an der Liechtensteinischen Ingenieurschule, Gastprofessuren an der Technischen Universität Graz und der Universität Ljubljana. Seit 2002 Professor für Holzbau an der Technischen Universität München. Zahlreiche Hallen für Zimmereien und andere Gewerbe zeugen von seinen zielgerichteten entwerferischen Konzepten für die Holztragwerke, die für Gemeindesäle architektonisch verfeinert ebenso wirksam sind. Neben mehreren Dutzend Einfamilienhäusern ergänzen zurückhaltende Erneuerungen alter Bausubstanz in empfindlichen Dorfstrukturen die Werkliste und belegen sein feines Gespür im Umgang mit der vorhandenen Baukultur und derLandschaft.

Christian Lenz

wurde 1952 in Wien geboren. Die Familie – die Mutter gebürtige Wienerin, der Vater Vorarlberger aus Hard – übersiedelte 1955 nach Dornbirn, wo er aufwuchs und am Realgymnasium maturierte. Archiekturstudium an der Technischen Universität Wien, Diplom 1981 bei Prof. Ernst Hiesmayr. 1982 Gründung des eigenen Architekturbüros in Schwarzach, Vorarlberg; ab 1983 in Bürogemeinschaft mit Hermann Kaufmann, 1986 mit Elmar Gmeiner, – 1993 auch Zusammenarbeit mit Helmut Dietrich. Plante er zu Beginn vor allem Einfamilienhäuser, folgten bald Industriehallen, die Seilbahnstation Griessenkareck in Wagrein/Salzburg sowie mehrere Gemeindesäle. Die erneuernde Transformation der Kirchen Lustenau und Tisis mit Hermann Kaufmann und Helmut Dietrich sowie jene für das Gymnasium Mehrerau erweiterten das Tätigkeitsgebiet. Mehrere Wohnanlagen, das Apartementhaus in Warth, der neue Innenausbau der MS Vorarlberg und das Zahnambulatorium in Bregenz sowie zahlreiche Umbauten und Sanierungen zeugen von einem breitgefächerten Feld architektonisch anspruchsvoll gelöster Bauaufgaben, in denen ein differenzierteres Materialgefühl und die Liebe zum Detail stark spürbar sind.

Walter Zschokke

wurde 1948 in Wildegg /Schweiz geboren; Architekturstudium an der ETH Zürich; Baupraxis. 1977 – 85 Assistent bei Prof. A. M. Vogt, ETH Zürich; Doktorat in Architekturgeschichte. Seit 1985 in Wien tätig auf dem Gebiet der Architektur als Entwerfer, Kritiker, Historiker, Kurator und Ausstellungsgestalter. 1989 gemeinsames Atelier mit Architekt Walter Hans Michl: Stadthaus in Wien-Neubau, Kirchenzentrum St. Benedikt in Wien-Simmering, Neueinrichtung Technisches Museum Wien, Mehrfamilienhaus und Einfamilienhaus in Aarau /Schweiz. Ausstellungskonzept und wissenschaftliche Leitung der Steirischen Landesausstellung 1995, „Holzzeit". Buchpublikationen: u.a. Adolf Krischanitz, Rüdiger Lainer, Dietrich/Untertrifaller, Jüngling / Hagmann, „Die Sustenstraße", „Architektur in Niederösterreich 1986 – 97". Zahlreiche Beiträge für Fachzeitschriften und Ausstellungskataloge; seit 1988 Architekturkritiker für die Wochenendbeilage ‚Spectrum', ‚Die Presse' Wien

Hermann Kaufmann

was born in 1955 in Reuthe, Bregenzerwald and grew up as the member of a well-known family in the carpentry business. His brother Michael runs the carpentry shop they inherited from the grandfather and father. After completing his secondary school education and receiving his Matura from the Bundesgymasium in Bregenz, Kauffman went on to study architecture at the Technical University in Innsbruck and Vienna. He rounded off his training with internships under the architects Leopold Kaufmann and Arch. Prof. Ernst Hiesmayr. He started his own office with Christian Lenz in Schwarzach in 1983. He has also taught at the Lichtenstein School of Engineering and has been a visiting professor the Graz Technical University and the University of Ljubljana, Slovenia. He has been a professor of timber construction at the Munich Technical University since 2002. A great number of halls for carpentry workshops and other business are proof that his purpose-oriented designs for timber supporting structures that are also adequate for community halls in their more refined forms. Dozens of single-family houses and restrained refurbishments of old buildings in sensitive village contexts on the project list show his fine sense for existing architectural culture and the landscape.

Christian Lenz

was born in Vienna in 1952. The family, his mother was Viennese-born, and his fther was from Hard in Vorarlberg, moved to Dornbirn in 1955, where Lenz grew up and completed his secondary school education. He studied architecture at the Vienna Technical University and received his degree in 1981, under Prof. Ernst Hiesmayr. He started his won office in Schwarzach, Vorarlberg in 1982. He began his ccoperation with Hermann Lenz and Elmar Gmeiner in 1983. He collaborated with Helmut Dietrich from 1986 until 1993. Initially, he mainly designed single-family houses. Soon, his activities also included industrial halls, the Greissenkareck in Wagrain/Salzburg as well as a number of community halls. The renewal and transformation of the churches in Lustenau and Tisis along with Hermann Kaufmann and Helmut Dietrich as well as the the Mehrerau Secondary School represent a further expansion of his architectural scope. A number of residential projects, the Warth Apartment House, the renovation of the interiors of the MS Vorarlberg and of those of the Bregenz Dental Clinic are examples of a broad spectrum of challenging architectural solutions. His love of detail and his fine sense of differentiation in terms of construction materials help secure a good place for his work within Vorarlberg's architectural landscape.

Walter Zschokke

was born in Wildegg, Switzerland in 1948. He studied architecture at the ETH, Zurich. Experience: he served as an assistant to Prof. A.M. Vogt, ETH Zurich from 1977 until 1985 before completeing his doctorate in architectural history. He has worked in Vienna since 1985 as an architecture designer, critic, historian, curator and exhibition designer. He started a joint architecture office with Hans Michl in 1989. Projects: townhouse in Vienna's 7th district, St. Benedict Church Center in the 11th district, refurbishment of the Vienna Technical Museum, apartment and single-family house projects in Aarau, Switzerland. He was also responsible for the for exhibition concept and research leadership for the Styrian Country Fair/ "Holzzeit" (Timber Time) in 1995. Publications: in conjunction with Adolf Krischanitz, Rüdiger Lainer, Dietrich Untertrifaller, Jüngling/Hagmann, "Die Sustenstrasse", Architektur in Niederösterreich 1986-1997. He has also submitted a number of contributions for architectural journals and exhibition catalogues. He has worked as the architecture critic for the Spectrum weekend supplement of the Viennese daily Die Presse since 1988.

Das Werk ist urheberrechtlich geschützt. Die dadurch begründeten Rechte, insbesondere die der Übersetzung, des Nachdruckes, der Entnahme von Abbildungen, der Funksendung, der Wiedergabe auf photomechanischem oder ähnlichem Wege und der Speicherung in Datenverarbeitungsanlagen, bleiben, auch bei nur auszugsweiser Verwertung, vorbehalten.

This work is subject to copyright. All rights are reserved, whether the whole or part of the material is concerned, specifically those of translation, reprinting, re-use of illustrations, broadcasting, reproduction by photocopying machines or similar means, and storage in data banks.

© 2002 Springer-Verlag/Wien

Printed in Austria

Die Wiedergabe von Gebrauchsnamen, Handelsnamen, Warenbezeichnungen usw. in diesem Buch berechtigt auch ohne besondere Kennzeichnung nicht zu der Annahme, daß solche Namen im Sinne der Warenzeichen- und Markenschutz-Gesetzgebung als frei zu betrachten wären und daher von jedermann benutzt werden dürften.

The use of registered names, trademarks, etc. in this publication does not imply, even in the absence of specific statement, that such names are exempt from the relevant protective laws and regulations and therefore free for general use.

Herausgeber und Autor | Editor & author
Walter Zschokke

Projektkoordination | Project management
Gabriele Hockauf

Übersetzung | Translation
Pedro M. López

Konzept und Gestaltung | Concept and design
Bohatsch Visual Communication, Wien

Druck | Printing
A. Holzhausens Nfg., A-1140 Wien

Gedruckt auf säurefreiem, chlorfrei gebleichtem Papier – TCF
Printed on acid-free and chlorine-free bleached paper

SPIN: 10725466

Bibliografische Information der Deutschen Bibliothek
Die Deutsche Bibliothek verzeichnet diese Publikation in der Deutschen Nationalbibliografie; detaillierte bibliografische Daten sind im Internet über <http://dnb.ddb.de> abrufbar.

Mit zahlreichen (teilweise farbigen) Abbildungen
With numerous (partly coloured) Figures

ISBN 3-211-83309-9
Springer-Verlag Wien New York

Fotografie | Photography
Ignacio Martinez, Lustenau
Seite | Page Titelfoto, 1, 11, 12, 13, 15, 17, 18, 19, 21, 22/23, 29, 30, 32, 33, 34, 36, 38, 39, 45, 46, 47, 49, 50, 51, 52, 53, 54, 75, 77, 79, 81, 83, 85, 87, 89, 91, 92, 93, 94, 95, 97, 98, 99, 100, 101, 103, 104, 105, 106, 107, 109, 110, 119, 121, 123, 124, 125, 127, 128, 129, 131, 132, 133, 134, 137, 138, 139, 140, 141, 143, 144, 145, 147, 148, 149, 157, 158, 159, 163, 164, 165, 167, 168, 169, 171, 172, 173, 174, 175, 177, 178, 179, 180, 187, 188, 189, 191, 193, 194, 195, 197, 198, 200, 207
im Werksverzeichnis 8, 9, 10, 11, 12, 13, 14, 16, 18, 19, 21, 22, 23, 24
Myrzik & Jarisch, München
Seite | Page 25, 26, 61, 62, 63, 65
im Werksverzeichnis 3
Foto Felder, Mellau
Seite | Page 5
Helmut Brunner
Seite | Page 199
Familie Geissler
Seite | Page 187 (kl.)
Christian Lenz
Seite | Page 45 (kl.), 160, 16
im Werksverzeichnis 1, 17
Hermann Kaufmann
Seite | Page 57, 59, 29 (kl.)
im Werksverzeichnis 2, 4, 6, 7, 15
Edi Hueber, New York
Seite | Page 27
Paul Ott, Graz
Seite | Page 67, 68
Adolf Bereuter, Lauterach
Seite | Page 41, 42/43, 183, 184, 185
im Werksverzeichnis 20
Bruno Klomfar, Wien
Seite | Page 71, 72, 73, 113, 114, 116, 117
Hajo Willig
Seite | Page 153, 154, 155